HELPS FOR TRANSLATORS

Volume XV

A TRANSLATOR'S HANDBOOK

on

THE BOOK OF

RUTH

by

JAN DE WAARD

and

EUGENE A. NIDA

UNITED BIBLE SOCIETIES

London

CM-BR3788-6/73-1M-08518

PREFACE

This Handbook on Ruth employs the same new format that was used in the recently published Handbook on Romans. The running text is again in Today's English Version, and it appears twice: first in larger sections, so as to provide a basis for comments on various aspects of the discourse structure; and then again in a verse-by-verse arrangement, so that the reader may be able to refer readily to the full form of a verse while reading the explanations of the various difficulties in it. This double reproduction of the running text follows a recommendation of the United Bible Societies' Committee on Translator's Helps, a recommendation which was made in answer to requests from persons who had used earlier volumes in the series and felt that this type of format would be an improvement.

The running text consists of the Stage II of the TEV. This is not necessarily the final form of this text, since it is subject to modification before the TEV Old Testament is published in 1976. But further alterations in the TEV text of Ruth are likely to be relatively minor. Though the TEV is used as a running text and hence constitutes a basis for various comments on discourse structure and translational difficulties, the Handbook is prepared essentially on the basis of the Hebrew text itself, even as the numerous comments and especially the notes make abundantly clear.

This Handbook differs from others in the considerable number of technical notes which are included in the Appendix. These notes not only contain discussions of special exegetical problems but provide valuable bibliographical references.

The authors of this Handbook wish to acknowledge the very important help which they have received from various members of the UBS Committee on Translator's Helps who have read the manuscript and have supplied many extremely useful observations and criticisms.

Jan de Waard
Eugene A. Nida

March 1973

[v]

CONTENTS

TRANSLATING THE BOOK OF RUTH

The Book of Ruth has consistently been one of the most popular stories of the Old Testament. It is often the first book translated into so-called "new languages," not only because the content of the story proves to be so interesting, but because the narrative develops in a relatively clear and easy manner. Furthermore, the Hebrew is not particularly difficult, and there are not many textual complications. Perhaps one of the reasons why the Book of Ruth is one of the first books to be dealt with by Old Testament translators is that it is one of the first books to be studied in classes in Hebrew.

Translating the Book of Ruth would be easier if we possessed certain clues as to the time when it was written, but there are no clear clues either in the content or in the forms of language which would indicate when this story was composed. (See Note 1.)* The frequent repetition of the term "Moabitess" in connection with Ruth has led to the suggestion that perhaps this book was written in the time of Ezra and Nehemiah as a protest against the stern measures taken by these leaders against men who had married Moabite wives, but there is really nothing substantive either in the grammatical forms, the choice of vocabulary, or reference to historical events which can tell us precisely when this book was written. We do know, of course, that it was written after the time of David and probably several centuries after the time of "the judges," for not only does the writer refer back to the time of the judges (1.1), but he explicitly refers to customs which were presumably followed in earlier times, but had been altered or abandoned by the time of the writing (4.7).

Not only do we lack clear evidence concerning the time of the writing of the Book of Ruth, but the purpose or purposes of this composition are likewise not evident. There are a number of significant themes, such as God's ultimate faithfulness, loyalty between persons, and the importance of clan relations, especially in the act of redeeming one's title to property. Since these various themes do have wide application, and since similar concepts and attitudes exist in many societies, the Book of Ruth has been greatly appreciated. It seems to speak so well to the needs and interests of people in many societies throughout the world.

The basic narrative structure of this book has been described by some as illustrating the theme of "from emptiness to fullness"; that is to say, the chief characters of the story begin with nothing and end with abundance.[2] This fundamental theme has sometimes been described simply as "from poverty to riches." In the very first section (1.1-5) the theme of "emptiness" is introduced, and it is made even more explicit in the second section (1.6-21). In the last verse of this section Naomi states "the Lord has brought me back empty," or, "the Lord has brought me back without a thing."

After the transitional verse 1.22, which, in a sense, sets the stage for change, the theme of "fullness" begins. It is seen first in chapter 2, where Ruth

---

*The notes appear near the end of this volume, beginning on page 83. Hereafter they will be referred to by superior (raised) figures, as (2).

[1]

gleans a large quantity of barley. Good fortune is expanded in chapter 3, where Ruth receives the promise of acceptance by her kinsman Boaz, as well as twice the amount of barley that she had gleaned earlier. The next section (4.1-12) constitutes the legal enactment of the promise made in chapter 3 and ends with the hope of children, which would, of course, be the culminating event of fullness for both Naomi and Ruth. The last section (4.13-17) confirms the blessing in the birth of the child Obed.

In keeping with the theme "from emptiness to fullness," the narrative development of the Book of Ruth is relatively simple. It consists essentially of seven closely related parts: (1) introduction or setting (1.1-5); (2) return (1.6-22); (3) gleaning (2.1-23); (4) acceptance by Boaz (3.1-18); (5) legal procedures (4.1-12); (6) the birth of Obed (4.13-17); and (7) conclusion, consisting of a brief genealogy (4.18-22). Section 5, legal procedures, is an elaboration of the promise made in section 4; and section 7, the conclusion, is an elaboration of the final statement in 4.17, which relates Obed to Jesse and then to David. To some persons the genealogy in 4.18-22, which goes from Perez to David, would seem to be an anticlimax or "letdown," but for the people of Israel this concluding genealogy would be a fitting and effective climax to the narrative.

There are two brief transitional sections in this story. One is 1.22, which consists of a summary of the preceding chapter, meanwhile introducing what will happen in the following chapter, namely, Ruth's gleaning during the barley harvest. Verse 4.7 is likewise a type of transition, for it summarizes certain aspects of what has already been mentioned in 4.1-6, while at the same time introducing the episode involving the removal of the sandal in 4.8-10.

For the translator of the Book of Ruth there are several types of problems which need to be given very careful consideration. These involve primarily cultural differences, use of direct discourse, plays on words, references to persons, and transitional devices.

Several of the "cultural specialities" referred to in the Book of Ruth may seem very strange to people in a number of societies: for example, returning to the house of one's mother (1.8), gleaning heads of grain behind the reapers (2.3), threshing by beating out the grain (2.17), levirate marriage (1.11-13), and legal procedures in redemption by a kinsman (4.1-11). In a number of cases it is necessary to have supplementary notes to provide the necessary background so that the reader will understand the story; otherwise the event will seem abnormally strange and the behavior of the participants almost meaningless.

Direct discourse is a very important feature of the Book of Ruth. In fact, it occupies fifty-five of the eighty-five verses of the book. Fortunately, there is very little discourse within discourse, such as occurs so frequently, for example, in Isaiah and Jeremiah. There are, however, several instances in which special attention must be given to introductory expressions for direct discourse; for example, in 1.19 a question would probably demand in many languages some introductory verb, such as "they asked one another" or, perhaps, "they exclaimed." In certain instances the reference with a direct quotation may be difficult to identify; for example, in 3.14, if Boaz is speaking directly to Ruth, then the reference should be "you," rather than "she" (TEV) or "the woman" (RSV). There are other minor problems involving direct discourse, but these will be discussed as they occur at various points throughout the text.

There are also certain problems of translation where there is a play on the meanings of words, particularly the proper names Naomi and Mara. To some extent Mara is explained within the text itself (1.20), but this reference may not be completely clear to the reader, and supplementary notes concerning the meaning of both Naomi and Mara are usually necessary.

The problems of reference in the Book of Ruth are generally not so difficult as is often the case in the Old Testament, but there are some which do present difficulties. For example, the reference to "the judges" assumes that the reader knows about the judges. This would be true of any Hebrew reader, but it surely would not be true of the average present-day reader. Likewise, in 1.19 "the women" must be identified in some languages so that the reference may not be misleading. In some languages it would appear strange that the next of kin referred to in chapter 4 is not named; everyone else is explicitly named, but this next of kin is only referred to by a phrase. This produces difficulties for the translator, particularly if an equivalent of "the next of kin" turns out to be a rather involved phrase or clause.

There are a number of transitional devices in the Book of Ruth—expressions which hold the story together and mark the transition from one episode, or part of the story, to another. For example, the reference to the barley harvest in 1.22 is an important transition, since it serves to introduce the gleaning of the barley in the following chapter. Likewise, Naomi's words in 3.18, "until he settles the matter," suggest that the very next part of the story will concern the legal procedures. Note also how 4.12, which contains the conclusion of the elders, anticipates the account of the birth of Obed in 4.13-15.

In addition to these transitions which are marked by content, there are certain transitional particles. Note, for example, the use of "then" in the TEV text of 1.22 and 3.1. The conjunction "so" occurs to introduce paragraphs in 3.6 and 4.13 (TEV). There are a number of other transitional particles which occur between sentences. All of these should be carefully matched by appropriate equivalents in the receptor language.

Undoubtedly the Book of Ruth contains one of the best structured and most delightful stories of the Old Testament. It is important, therefore, that the translator do justice to both the form and the content of this narrative, so that it can be fully appreciated by the many readers who will hopefully find not only pleasure but spiritual guidance and encouragement from this ancient account.

[3]

CHAPTER 1

Elimelech and His Family in Moab

1 In the days before Israel had a king, there was a famine in the country. So a man from Bethlehem, in the territory of Judah, took his wife and two sons and went to live for a while in the country of Moab. ²The man's name was Elimelech, his wife was Naomi, and their two sons were Mahlon and Chilion. They belonged to the clan of Ephrath. While they were living in Moab, ³Elimelech died, and Naomi was left alone with her two sons. ⁴They married Moabite girls: one was named Orpah, the other Ruth. After they had lived there about ten years, ⁵Mahlon and Chilion also died, and Naomi was left all alone, without her two sons and her husband.

As has already been mentioned, this first section (1.1-5) constitutes the introduction to the book. It provides all the necessary information for the following story, since it describes the time, place, persons, and circumstance (namely, the famine) which gave rise to the events described later in the book. The theme of "emptiness" is particularly emphasized in this section by the mention of "a famine in the country" (1.1), the death of Elimelech (1.3), and finally the deaths of Mahlon and Chilion (1.5). All of this is summarized in the expression Naomi was left all alone, without her two sons and her husband. This theme of "emptiness" begins, therefore, with a natural catastrophe, the famine, and ends with personal catastrophe, the loss of all of Naomi's immediate family.

It is difficult to select a title for this first section of the Book of Ruth. The expression Elimelech and His Family in Moab does not do full justice to what follows, but if one wishes to use an expression such as "A Famine Forces Elimelech and His Family to Go to Moab," this may prove to be unduly long and perhaps even confusing, since Moab might be interpreted as a person rather than a place. Some translators prefer simply to use the title "Naomi and Ruth" as a section heading for the entire first chapter. This has distinct advantages, even though Ruth is mentioned in only a limited way in this first section. A quite different title might be employed, such as "Tragedy Comes to the Family of Elimelech" or "The Family of Elimelech Suffers Much"—provided, of course, that "suffer" does not imply literal physical suffering, but simply the undergoing of tragic events.

1.1   In the days before Israel had a king, there was a famine in the country. So a man from Bethlehem, in the territory of Judah, took his wife and two sons and went to live for a while in the country of Moab.

The initial clause, in the days before Israel had a king, provides the setting of time for the following story, but there are certain complications in the expression used in the original text. The Hebrew has literally "when the judges judged." This becomes doubly confusing since "the judges" would seem to imply old information. This would, of course, be true for the Jews who would read the story; but it is essential that some modification of this expression be made in a number of receptor languages. An additional difficulty occurs in the use of the term "judges," since in many societies it may seem quite anomalous to have a judge ruling. The task of ruling exists with executive power and not with judicial authority. In reality, of course, the judges of the Old Testament were essentially like "chiefs" in many present-day societies. They not only judged differences between people, but they were primarily the leaders who gave direction to the life of Israel.[1] Accordingly, in many languages it is necessary to render this first clause as "during the time when chiefs ruled the country of Israel" or "...the people of Israel." To express duration of time one may also say in some languages: "when judges were ruling the country of Israel." Such an expression may eliminate the necessity for a general expression such as "during the time when." The historical period could be marked as it is done in the TEV, in the days before Israel had a king. However, as the words for "chief" and "king" are identical in many receptor languages, this might create the impression that at that time there were no chiefs in Israel, which, of course, would be wrong.

In English the expression there was a famine is a way of introducing famine as new information, but in many languages there is simply no noun for famine; rather some verb expression must be employed, for example, "the people had nothing to eat." It is often important to indicate that the famine was the result of a natural catastrophe rather than merely that the people had run out of food because they did not plan properly. In some languages, therefore, one must say: "because of drought the people had nothing to eat."

The phrase in the country may need to be made somewhat more specific (for example, "in that country") so as to refer back specifically to "the country of Israel."[2] In certain instances, however, it is not necessary to indicate explicitly the place, since this may have already been introduced in the first clause, "when chiefs ruled the country of Israel." One may either omit the specific reference to country or employ a pronominal expression such as "there."

The particle translated by so constitutes an important transitional device to show the relationship between the famine mentioned in the first sentence and the decision of Elimelech to go with his family to the country of Moab. In some languages this transition may be made even more explicit: "as a result" or "because of this famine."

In a number of languages it is quite awkward to speak of the activity of a man and after that introduce information concerning his wife and two sons who were with him. It may be preferable to translate: "so a man, together with his wife and two sons, went...."

An even more disturbing element, as far as the discourse structure of this introduction is concerned, is the fact that a man is mentioned together with his wife and two sons, and then only later are the names of the various persons given. This may seem particularly awkward, since the first part of verse 2 may need to be coalesced with the second sentence of verse 1 to read: "So a man from Bethlehem named Elimelech, together with his wife Naomi and their two sons Mahlon and Chilion, went to live for a while in the country of Moab."

In some instances it may be useful to employ a classifier with Bethlehem, so that it may be identified as a "town" in the territory of Judah.

[6]

The country of Moab would normally be understood as the plateau of Moab, which is slightly higher than the mountainous country of Judah. To go to the country of Moab Elimelech and his family would need to descend into the Jordan valley and ascend the other side. The Hebrew term "country" is normally used to designate the whole territory of a certain tribe.3,4

The expression went to live for a while represents a rather technical Hebrew term to designate dwelling in some place for an indefinite amount of time as a newcomer and without original rights.5 It does not mean that Elimelech moved to Moab to stay there permanently; he was simply concerned about escaping temporarily the consequences of the famine which had taken place in Judah.

1.2   The man's name was Elimelech, his wife was Naomi, and their two sons were Mahlon and Chilion. They belonged to the clan of Ephrath. While they were living in Moab,

The proper names Elimelech, Naomi, Mahlon, and Chilion do have possible meanings in Hebrew. For example, Elimelech sounds like "God is King," Naomi, like "my pleasantness" (compare the note on 1.20), Mahlon, like "illness," and Chilion, like "consumption."6 These proper names are not found elsewhere in the Old Testament, but they should be treated simply as proper names and not as symbolic designations. In other words, they should be transliterated rather than translated, and this means that, in general, they should be adapted to the kinds of sounds which occur in the receptor language. The basis for the adaptation may be either Hebrew or some modern language dominant in the area. In a number of instances the form of proper names has already been decided by long practice, and modification is therefore extremely difficult, particularly if Naomi is in current use as a proper name.7 In all instances of transliterating, the translator must be careful that the form of the proper name does not sound like some receptor language word having a vulgar meaning.

It is extremely difficult to know precisely what is meant in the reference the clan of Ephrath. Several different solutions have been proposed, of which three seem to have the widest acceptance: (1) this is merely a designation of the inhabitants of the country around Bethlehem;8 (2) the phrase identifies "Ephrathah" with Bethlehem (compare Micah 5.2*); that is to say, "the Ephrathites" is only another way of talking about the inhabitants of Bethlehem itself;9 and (3) the phrase designates a clan of Judah which lived in Bethlehem.10 Since there is no special evidence for the first solution, and since the second solution appears to be a feature of later history, the third solution is probably to be preferred.

While they were living in Moab is a repetition of what has already been stated in verse 1. It is, however, more acceptable in the Hebrew text since the names of the members of the family are given in verse 2, and then a further reference to their relation to Bethlehem, the clan of Ephrath, is introduced. Therefore, before talking about the death of Elimelech in verse 3, it is necessary to

* Micah 5.1 in the Hebrew text.

repeat the fact that he had gone with his family to Moab. However, if the identification of the people by means of proper names (the first sentence of verse 2)
is coalesced with the second sentence of verse 1, it may be unnecessary and
even misleading to repeat the information concerning their going to Moab and
living there. Accordingly, in some languages this clause is omitted.

1.3-4a   Elimelech died, and Naomi was left alone with her two sons.
          (4a) They married Moabite girls: one was named Orpah, the
          other Ruth.

The Hebrew text of verse 3 reads "Elimelech the husband of Naomi died,
and she was left with her two sons." The expression "the husband of Naomi" is
so repetitious of the information already given in verse 2 as to appear almost
misleading. Therefore, in some translations (as here) the phrase is omitted,
and in place of the pronoun "she" the name Naomi is used. One may actually
transfer the expression "the husband of Naomi" to the second part of verse 3
and read: "and Naomi, his wife, was left with her two sons."

The Hebrew expression translated Naomi was left may be rendered in certain contexts as "she was left behind" or "she was left alive,"[11] but in many languages it is extremely difficult to translate the Hebrew verb literally. (Compare
French elle lui survécut.[12]) The translator must select a natural equivalent in
the receptor language to designate a woman who is left as a widow with two sons,
for example, "Naomi, his wife, was left a widow with her two sons," "Naomi
remained alone with her two sons," or "Naomi no longer had a husband, only
her two sons."

The Hebrew expression here translated married occurs only in Old Testament literature of a later period.[13] It is true that the same expression does occur in Judges 21.23, but it is in a context which concerns the abduction of women,
literally in the sense of "to take wives." As such, the expression carries an important component of sex, not only in Hebrew but also in many receptor languages.

In Hebrew the proper name Orpah sounds like "rebellious" and Ruth sounds
like "friend." Etymologists have speculated considerably concerning possible
implications of the use of these names, but there is no certainty as to the historical background or the meaning.[14]

1.4b-5   After they had lived there about ten years, (5) Mahlon and Chilion
          also died, and Naomi was left all alone, without her two sons and her
          husband.

After they had lived there about ten years is a reference to the time that
Mahlon and Chilion lived in Moab—in other words, the time that the family had
been there. The ten years should not be counted from the time of Elimelech's
death.

The Hebrew verb translated was left is the same as occurs in verse 3. It
may, however, be useful to modify somewhat this last clause of verse 5 to introduce all of the component parts, but in a somewhat different arrangement, for

example, "Naomi lost her two sons and her husband and was thus left all alone."

Chronologically, Elimelech died first and Mahlon and Chilion afterward. It may be important, therefore, to reverse the order of without her two sons and her husband, as some ancient versions have done,[15] so that the phrase reads: "without her husband and her two sons." In addition, there may be a cultural reason in some languages to mention the husband before the sons.

Naomi and Ruth Return to Bethlehem

[6]While still in Moab, Naomi heard that the Lord had blessed his people by giving them good crops; so she got ready to leave Moab with her daughters-in-law. [7]They started out together to go back to Judah, [8]but on the way, she said to them, "Go back home, and stay with your mothers. May the Lord be as good to you as you have been to me and to those who have died. [9]And may the Lord make it possible for each of you to marry again and have a home."

So Naomi kissed them good-bye. But they started crying [10]and said to her, "No! We will go with you to your people."

[11]"You must go back, my daughters," Naomi answered. "Why do you want to come with me? Can I still have sons for you to marry? [12]Go back home; I am too old to get married again. Even if I thought there was still hope, and got married tonight and had sons, [13]would you wait to marry until they had grown up? Would this keep you from marrying someone else? My daughters, you know it's impossible. The Lord has turned against me, and I feel very sorry for you."

[14]Again they started crying. Then Orpah kissed her mother-in-law good-bye, but Ruth would not leave. [15]So Naomi said to her, "Ruth, your sister-in-law has gone back to her people and to her god. Go back home with her."

These paragraphs (1.6- 15) begin the second section of the Book of Ruth and describe the return of Naomi and Ruth to Bethlehem. The section concludes with a summary paragraph, verse 22. Verses 1-15 deal with Naomi and her relationship to Orpah and Ruth, while verses 15-18 are concerned with Ruth. Verses 19-21 describe the reaction of the people in Bethlehem to Naomi and her response. Though a number of translations employ only one paragraph for verses 6 through 21, it is generally more convenient and effective to break the passage into several paragraphs, and thus to separate the different aspects of Naomi's return.

The section heading Naomi and Ruth Return to Bethlehem is probably the most convenient and simple title which can be employed. However, it may be useful to emphasize the role of Ruth in this particular section, and therefore the section heading may be altered to read "Ruth Returns to Bethlehem with Naomi." In some languages, however, there is a problem involved in the verb return, for it would imply that both individuals had been in Bethlehem before, but only Naomi had been there. Therefore, in some languages one may have to say: "Naomi Returns to Bethlehem, and Ruth Goes with Her."

[9]

1.6   While still in Moab, Naomi heard that the Lord had blessed his
people by giving them good crops; so she got ready to leave Moab
with her daughters-in-law.

In the Hebrew text of verse 6 the preparation of Naomi to return with her
daughters-in-law comes before the statement with regard to the provision of
food in Judah. However, as in the TEV and many other translations, it is probably preferable to reverse the Hebrew order and follow the chronological sequence: (1) Naomi hears that the Lord has given his people good crops, and
therefore (2) she gets ready to leave Moab.

In using the rendering Lord, the TEV follows the practice of many modern
versions (for example, NEB and NAB) which reflects the Jewish custom of avoiding the pronunciation of the name of God, written in Hebrew with the four letters
YHWH. Because the personal name of God, Yahweh, was regarded as being such
a powerful word (technically, a matter of positive taboo[16]), Jewish people always read the Scriptures by substituting the more familiar and common term
Adonai. Evidence for this substitution is found in the points which were put with
the Hebrew consonants to indicate the vowels of Adonai.

Some translators simply transliterate the name Yahweh,[17] while others
employ a transliteration of the traditional term Jehovah, which reflects a pronunciation introduced by Galatinus in 1520. A few translators seek to interpret
the meaning of Yahweh by using some such expression as der Ewige (Buber-
Rosenzweig), l'Eternel (Segond), or "the Eternal" (Moffatt). Such translations
are rather speculative in character, and they tend to introduce a rather imper-
sonal aspect into the rendering of this personal name. Accordingly, translators
are advised to follow the practice which began as early as the Greek Septuagint
translation of the Old Testament, made some two hundred years before Christ,
in which Yahweh was normally rendered as Kurios "Lord." It may, of course,
be necessary in some languages to use a possessed form of "Lord," depending
on context, such as "her Lord," "their Lord," "my Lord," etc.

The rendering of Yahweh by "Lord" results in the Lord of the Old Testament being spoken of in the same way as Jesus Christ is addressed in the New
Testament. This is precisely the tradition which was used by the New Testament
writers. This translation seems to be fully justified in light of what has happened
in the history of the church.

The term blessed represents a Hebrew word which is often translated as
"visit," a Hebrew word which has two quite distinct meanings: (1) "to care for"
(e.g. Genesis 21.1; Exodus 13.19; Isaiah 23.17) and (2) "to punish" (e.g. Isaiah
10.12; Jeremiah 9.25). This means that the visitation of the Lord is either for
benefit or for punishment. Obviously in this particular context it is the first
meaning which is involved. The expression by giving them good crops is literally in Hebrew "and gave them bread," but in this context "bread" is to be understood in the more general sense of "food."[18] On the other hand, if one should
translate "gave them food," it might appear as though the Lord came to his people to pass out food, as one might do to refugees. What happened was that the
drought had been broken, and as a result of adequate rain there were good crops.

It seems, therefore, more satisfactory to translate, as the TEV has done, by giving them good crops.

The expression she got ready to leave reflects a Hebrew construction which has two verbs closely combined, "she arose... she returned," but the meaning of the combined verbs is simply "she got ready to leave," "she prepared to leave," or "she began to leave." This problem of translation was fully recognized in one ancient version which rendered the two verbs as one, "then she returned."[19]

The second clause of verse 6 involves a typical Hebrew construction, literally, "then she arose, she and her daughters-in-law, and she returned," but this is very difficult to translate literally into another language.[20] The Hebrew construction does, however, indicate clearly that it is Naomi who takes the initiative.[21] For that reason, the TEV has the rendering so she got ready to leave Moab with her daughters-in-law.

Most languages have a technical term or designation for daughters-in-law. If such a term does not exist, one can always employ a descriptive phrase, such as "the wives of her sons," "the wives of her sons who had recently died," or "the widows of her sons."

1.7   They started out together to go back to Judah,

The Hebrew text of verse 7 is rather awkward to render literally, "so she set out from the place where she was, with her two daughters-in-law, and they went on the way to return to the land of Judah." Even some ancient versions have made adaptations of this Hebrew text in order to obtain a smoother rendering; for example, "she set out" is changed to "they set out," since obviously all of them went together.[22] The expression "on the way" is sometimes deleted, and in some instances the second part of verse 7 is omitted as being unnecessary information, since the data has already been implied in verse 6.[23] However, rather than delete the second part of verse 7, it is possible to combine it with verse 8 as the NAB does: "she and her two daughters-in-law left the place where they had been living. Then as they were on the road back to the land of Judah...." Note how the text is restructured in the TEV.

One of the problems involved in rendering verse 7 is that not all of the relevant information is given in the Hebrew text. From what follows later in chapter 1, it seems quite clear that Naomi did not invite her daughters-in-law to follow her. She apparently only informed them of her intentions of going, and they took the initiative to go along with her. In order to point out clearly that the conversation, beginning with verse 8, began only after the journey had started, the latter part of verse 7 can be conveniently rendered as to go back to Judah. Perhaps the actual conversation took place at the border between Moab and Judah in the Jordan valley.

1.8   but on the way, she said to them, "Go back home, and stay with your
         mothers. May the Lord be as good to you as you have been to me and
         to those who have died.

Stay with your mothers involves a rather surprising Hebrew expression
referring to "the mother's house"; that is to say, each daughter-in-law was instructed to return to her mother's house, not to the home of her father, which
one would normally expect (see, for example, Genesis 38.11; Leviticus 22.13;
Numbers 30.16; Deuteronomy 22.21; Judges 19.2,3). In fact, one ancient version has changed the text at this point to read "to the house of your father,"[24]
while another employs an easier reading, "to your country and to the house of
your parents."[25] These indicate that even early translators found difficulty with
the Hebrew text at this point. Some have argued that the reference to the mother's house was a way in which Naomi could keep open the possibility of the girls'
contracting marriage again without affecting their relationship to Israel. Presumably it would have been different if they had been sent back to "the house of
their fathers."[26] However, this argument is not very convincing. There is some
doubt, indeed, as to precisely the extent to which so-called levirate rights applied.[27] It may be that there is here a trace of some early matriarchal organization such as the ancient Arabs had, in which the tent was normally regarded
as the property of the wife.[28]

This expression "the mother's house" is not only a problem for exegesis
(that is, for determining what it meant in the Hebrew text); it poses the similarly difficult problem of interpretation in many receptor languages where it
would seem almost incredible that a woman would be sent back to her mother's
house, especially since she would presumably belong to the family of her husband. This means that for a number of receptor languages it is important to
have an explanatory marginal note, for example, "According to the custom of
the ancient Hebrews, a widow who had no children could either stay with the family of her deceased husband or could remarry outside of that family."

The second part of verse 8 begins a blessing which extends through the
first part of verse 9. This is then followed by the simple departure ceremony
of kissing (9b). The Hebrew term rendered be good to or have been [good] to
is frequently translated as "show kindness to," "be kind to," or "treat kindly."
The Hebrew term is the same one which is often rendered in the RSV as "stead-
fast love," and two of its basic components of meaning are loyalty and faithfulness.[29] Accordingly, the NEB has "may the Lord keep faith with you." However,
it is difficult to indicate this meaning of the Hebrew expression in this particular
context, since there is no setting which would suggest loyalty or faithfulness, except insofar as the Lord would "be good to" them, even as the daughters-in-law
had "been good to" Naomi and to those who had died.

In some languages the only satisfactory way of speaking about "being good
to someone" is to use a term such as "to help," for example, "may the Lord
help you as you have helped me and those who have died." But in many languages
one cannot use this form of request or blessing without employing some expression to introduce the direct quotation, for example, "I pray to the Lord that he

may be good to you..." or as addressed directly to God, "I ask you, Lord, Be good to my daughters-in-law as they have been good to me and to those who have died."

1.9-10 And may the Lord make it possible for each of you to marry again and have a home."
  So Naomi kissed them good-bye. But they started crying (10) and said to her, "No! We will go with you to your people."

The phrase make it possible (Hebrew: "give") may be rendered in a number of languages as a causative: "may the Lord cause you to marry again" or "may the Lord give you other husbands."[30]

The Hebrew word here rendered home literally means "resting place." It is often used as a technical military term, but it is also employed as a reference to the promised land (Deuteronomy 12.9; 1 Kings 8.56; Psalm 95.11) and to Zion as the place where Yahweh dwells (Psalm 132.8, 14). In this context the translation home is particularly appropriate, since the Hebrew word carries the meanings of peace and happiness as well as of security, all of which are regarded as the result of marriage (cf. 3.1). It is not enough to translate "have a house," since widows could possess houses. What is referred to here is a home with a husband. The equivalent in some languages is "to live in a house with your husband."

In some languages it is quite improper to translate Naomi kissed them, for kissing is regarded only as an expression of sexual interest or involvement. Under such circumstances one must use some such expression as "to embrace," "to place one's arms around," or "to hold tenderly."

Even when one can refer to kissing, it is sometimes necessary to mark the kissing as an expression of parting: Naomi kissed them good-bye and to introduce a verb of speaking before the term good-bye, for example, "so Naomi kissed them and said good-bye to them." In some languages the term for good-bye is quite idiomatic: "I leave my heart with you" or "until we see each other again," but in other languages the expression for good-bye is quite matter of fact, for example, "now I am leaving."

They started crying is literally in Hebrew "they lifted up their voices and wept." The idiom "to lift up the voice" can rarely be translated literally, and the combined expression in Hebrew simply means loud sobbing.[31]

It may be necessary to indicate in some languages that they in the last clause in verse 9 refers to the daughters-in-law, since it could presumably be a reference to Naomi as well as to her daughters-in-law, because of the deep emotional attachment. However, the beginning of verse 10 makes it quite clear that it is only the daughters-in-law who began to weep.

The translation of the negative No, which is implicit in the Hebrew text, is particularly difficult in some languages, for it might imply that they did not wish to receive the blessing which Naomi had given to them. That, of course, is not the meaning; and it may be necessary to expand the negative to read: "do not say good-bye to us" or "we do not wish to leave you."

[13]

The Hebrew text literally has "return" in the second clause of verse 10, but since the daughters-in-law did not really "return" to Judah (in the sense that they had been there before), it is better to employ some such expression as in the TEV, we will go with you.

In some languages to your people may be rendered most effectively as "to your tribe" or even "to your clan."

1.11   "You must go back, my daughters," Naomi answered. "Why do
            you want to come with me? Can I still have sons for you to marry?

You must go back represents an imperative expression in Hebrew. However, it should not be interpreted as a harsh command, but simply as strong advice. In some languages the closest equivalent would be "it is best for you to go back" or "you should go back."

One must make certain that my daughters is satisfactorily rendered to identify "daughters-in-law." In some languages a shift of terminology at this point could be very misleading.

The term answered is quite appropriate in English, but in some languages there are two different verbs, one used for answering a question and the other for responding to a statement. It is the latter meaning which is involved in this context.

Can I still have sons? is a rendering of a Hebrew idiom meaning literally "Have I yet sons in my womb?" (cf. Genesis 25.23 and Psalm 71.6[32]). One ancient translation changed the expression "in my womb" to something more euphemistic: "Do I yet have sons?"[33] It is also possible in this context to follow the rendering of the NEB: "Am I likely to bear any more sons to be husbands for you?" This is a direct reference to the levirate right, in which a man was obliged to marry the wife of his deceased brother. It may be necessary at this point to have an explanatory marginal note; otherwise, Naomi's rhetorical question may seem utterly foolish.

When a rhetorical question implies such a definite negative answer as the last question in verse 11, it is appropriate in a number of languages to indicate this fact, often by a negative phrase appended to or incorporated into the question, for example, "I couldn't still have sons for you to marry, could I?" In many languages, however, this type of rhetorical question must be changed into a negative statement, for example, "I certainly could not bear sons who would grow up and marry you."

1.12-13   Go back home; I am too old to get married again. Even if I thought
           there was still hope, and got married tonight and had sons, (13) would
           you wait to marry until they had grown up? Would this keep you from
           marrying someone else? My daughters, you know it's impossible. The
           Lord has turned against me, and I feel very sorry for you."

The expression go back home represents the combination of two Hebrew verbs often translated "turn back...go your way." These verbs do not repre-

[14]

sent two different movements, but simply emphasize the meaning of return-ing. [34,35]

In the Hebrew text of verse 12 there is no indication of a goal of hope (cf. NAB "and even if I could offer any hopes"). There are, of course, two different possibilities for a goal of hope, either the hope of marrying (Moffatt) or the hope of having a child (NEB). The more immediate element in the context would seem to be marrying or having a husband, but since the focus is not on the hus-band but on having sons, it is also possible to speak of "hope of having sons."

In the Hebrew text the expression rendered got married tonight is a more or less direct reference to the act of sexual intercourse, but it is euphemisti-cally stated. Some ancient translators, however, felt that it was not euphemis-tic enough and so they omitted "tonight."[36] Others, however, translated quite realistically.[37] In some languages the closest and most appropriate equivalent would be "even if I should sleep with a husband tonight"[38] or "even if a husband should cause me to conceive tonight."

The Hebrew term involved in the expression keep you from marrying oc-curs only here in the Old Testament though it is frequent in later rabbinic liter-ature.[39] In this particular context one might render the verb as "shut yourselves off from marrying" or "deprive yourselves of marrying."

Since the questions posed by Naomi in verse 13 are regarded not as real questions but as rhetorical exclamations of something which is quite impossible, it is frequently preferable to render them as strong negative statements, for ex-ample, "if I should have a husband tonight and then give birth to sons, you surely would not wait until they had grown up. You would not refrain from marrying someone else."

The clause you know it's impossible renders a negative particle in Hebrew which presupposes a verbal form which is not made explicit.[40] The negation may refer either to the impossibility of Naomi's having sons for her daughters-in-law to marry, or it may be a negative command advising the daughters not to accompany her.

The clause the Lord has turned against me occurs in the Hebrew text at the end of verse 13, following a clause which may have either of two meanings: (1) "I am terribly sorry for you" or (2) "my lot is worse than yours."[41] The RSV, NAB, and TEV follow the first interpretation, while Moffatt and the NEB favor the second. One can argue that because of the clause the Lord has turned against me the second interpretation is to be preferred, but that does not neces-sarily follow. If the order of clauses is reversed, as in the TEV, the meaning is quite clear and the relation between the events is logical, since it was evi-dently adversity brought on by the Lord which caused Naomi to feel so sorry for her daughters-in-law. This is, of course, a reference to the death of the two sons.

In the Hebrew text the phrase "the hand of the Lord" is a figurative expres-sion to identify the power of the Lord. In most instances it is better to drop this figure of speech and say simply the Lord has turned against me rather than "the hand of the Lord has gone against me."

[15]

1.14   Again they started crying. Then Orpah kissed her mother-in-law good-bye, but Ruth would not leave.

Though the term <u>again</u> seems necessary in view of the intervening statement by Naomi, the emphasis of the Hebrew word is upon the continuation of the weeping.[42] This meaning may be expressed as "they wept still more."

The phrase <u>started crying</u> reflects the same expressions occurring in 1.9, which in Hebrew is literally "lifted up their voices and wept."

Though the term for <u>kissed</u> in verse 14 is the same as in verse 9, it may be necessary to use some quite different expression, such as "embraced," because of the connotations of the word <u>kissed</u>. Furthermore, in some languages there may be a different term used because of the difference of social position between Orpah and Naomi.

There is almost always some technical term to designate <u>mother-in-law</u>, but if this does not exist, one can employ some descriptive expression, for example, "the mother of her husband," or, as in this context, "the mother of her deceased husband."

As in verse 9, it may be necessary to translate <u>kissed...good-bye</u> as "kissed and said good-bye."

At this point (that is, between <u>...good-bye,</u> and <u>but Ruth...</u>), the Septuagint adds "and she went back to her people."[43] This information is, of course, implicit in the Hebrew text, and in some cases it may be necessary to make this fact explicit in translation.

The expression <u>would not leave</u> is a translation of a Hebrew verb meaning "to cleave," and it has the figurative meaning of loyalty and affection, as well as the meaning of being close to something or someone. A translation such as "to stay with" (NAB) is rather weak, and something like "remained close to her" may be understood only in the physical sense. The TEV, therefore, uses a negative expression as a more effective equivalent.

1.15   So Naomi said to her, "Ruth, your sister-in-law has gone back to her people and to her god. Go back home with her."

The Hebrew text at the beginning of verse 15 has simply "and she said." However, it is important to indicate clearly the transition between this paragraph and what has preceded by introducing some such particle as <u>so</u>. It may also be necessary to specify the participants, both Naomi and Ruth,[44] as in the TEV.

In a number of languages <u>sister-in-law</u> is rendered as "co-wife," since in many societies the wives of brothers call each other "co-wives" or "co-spouses." In some instances one may have to use a descriptive expression, for example, "the wife of your husband's brother." In a number of languages there are two quite distinct expressions for <u>sister-in-law</u>, one term designating a brother's wife and the other term specifying the sister of one's wife. These quite distinct relations may be marked by entirely different terms.

In some languages one cannot speak of <u>her people</u> or <u>her god</u>, for one does not possess people or a god. The first expression may be rendered in some languages as "the tribe to which she belongs," "the people of which she is a part," or "the people with whom she is counted"; and her god may be rendered as "the god whom she worships" or "the god to whom she prays."

Though a few translations have "gods," there is no firm basis for using the plural. The god of the Moabites was Chemosh[45] (see 1 Kings 11.33).

In translating the term god one should generally use the most generic term for deity.[46] However, if one normally uses an expression such as "the Eternal Spirit" as a translation of "God," it would not be possible to use the same expression in this context. It might then be necessary to use some such expression as "the spirit whom she worships."

The expression Go back home with her is emphatic, and some ancient translations even have an additional expression emphasizing the return.[47] In order to show the relation between the advice to Ruth and what Orpah had already done, it may be useful to introduce an emphatic pronoun "you yourself should go back home with her."

> [16]But Ruth answered, "Don't ask me to leave you. Let me go with you. Wherever you go, I will go; wherever you live, I will live. Your people will be my people, and your God will be my God. [17]Wherever you die, I will die, and that is where I will be buried. May the Lord's worst punishment come upon me if I let anything but death separate me from you!"
> [18]When Naomi saw that Ruth was determined to go with her, she said nothing more.

These verses represent the second phase of Naomi's return to Judah and deal exclusively with the relationship between Naomi and Ruth. They include one of the most beautiful and touching statements of human loyalty in world literature and may be regarded as the literary high point of this book.

1.16-17   But Ruth answered, "Don't ask me to leave you. Let me go with you. Wherever you go, I will go; wherever you live, I will live. Your people will be my people, and your God will be my God. (17) Wherever you die, I will die, and that is where I will be buried. May the Lord's worst punishment come upon me if I let anything but death separate me from you!"

Verses 16 and 17 have a poetic structure. Verse 16 consists of three lines with a meter of 3 + 2, 3 + 3, and 2 + 2. Verse 17 consists also of three lines with a meter of 3 + 2, 3 + 2, and 3 + 2.[48] If one can reproduce the poetic effect of this passage, it is important to do so. However, the content itself does not provide the basis for what one so frequently finds in poetry, namely, figurative expressions in a very condensed formal structure. Rather, what is characteristic of this passage is the parallelism, so typical of most Hebrew poetry. Therefore, what one should attempt in rendering this passage is a kind of dignified prose which will emphasize the parallelism and provide a rhythmic effect.

Though this passage does focus upon Ruth's loyalty to Naomi, it goes much further in that it constitutes a declaration of Ruth's allegiance to the Jewish com-

munity, since she identifies herself with the people and the God of Naomi.[49]
Furthermore, she concludes this statement of identification with an oath in
which she calls upon the Lord to punish her if she in any way violates her pledge
of loyalty.

Rather than the simple verb "said," as in Hebrew, it may be useful to employ at the beginning of verse 16 a term meaning answered, which will indicate
that Ruth is now responding to what Naomi has just said to her.

The Hebrew term here translated ask often means "to meet" or "to encounter," but in this particular context it has the specific meaning of "to encounter with a request."[50] To an extent the English verb ask is rather a weak equivalent for the Hebrew term. Expressions such as "do not urge me" or "do not
beseech me" would probably be closer equivalents.

The Hebrew text has two verbs, "leave" and "return," both dependent on
an introductory verb often translated "entreat," so that a traditional translation
is "do not entreat me to leave you or to return from following you." In the TEV
this structure is divided into two clauses, one with a negative command and the
other with a positive request: Don't ask me to leave you. Let me go with you.

In a number of languages wherever you go or wherever you live must be
expressed as a type of condition, for example, "If you go some place, I will go
there; and if you live some place, I will live there." In still other languages a
paratactic construction is sometimes employed, for example, "You will go some
place, then I will go there too; you will go to live some place, then I will go and
live there too."

For a treatment of the possessive pronoun with terms for people and God,
see the comments on verse 15. The very emphatic form of this declaration may
require the use of certain adverbial attributives, such as "certainly," "surely,"
"indeed," etc., for example, "your people will certainly be my people."

The clause that is where I will be buried probably does not seem too important to the average modern reader, but to people in many cultures this is one
of the most important expressions in the entire declaration of Ruth. For the sake
of some special advantage people may be willing to go and live among another
tribe or people, but they almost always want to be buried in their homeland.
Hence, it is this final statement of Ruth's which confirms her lasting loyalty.
In some languages it is difficult to have a passive expression will be buried.
Therefore, an indefinite active expression may sometimes be employed: "they
will bury me" or even "your people will bury me." Sometimes this concept may
be expressed euphemistically: "there my body will remain."

The last sentence of verse 17 consists of an oath and curse formula. In
Hebrew it is literally "may the Lord do so to me and more also," a formula
found in the Old Testament twelve times, once here and eleven times in the books
of Samuel and Kings (1 Samuel 3.17; 14.44; 20.13; 25.22; 2 Samuel 3.9,35; 19.13;
1 Kings 2.23; 2 Kings 6.31). A plural form of the verbs occurs in 1 Kings 19.2
and 20.10. In this particular formula, the expression translated "so" is a substitute for a curse which would normally be pronounced to indicate the nature of
the punishment, for example, sickness, loss of wealth, death.[51] It is rare that
in a receptor language one can use such an indefinite reference to the nature of

the curse or punishment; and therefore in the TEV a somewhat general statement is employed: May the Lord's worst punishment come upon me. Or one may follow Moffatt's translation: "May the Eternal kill me...." The NEB does not employ the curse formula, but it does indicate that an oath is involved: "I swear a solemn oath before the Lord your God." Many languages have set formulas for such vows and curses, for example, "May the anger of the Lord be upon me" or "May the curses come upon my head."[52] Whether or not one wishes to retain a literal translation of the Hebrew in a marginal note depends upon the extent to which an adaptation of this formula is required in the receptor language.

If I let anything but death represents a Hebrew expression which may be translated literally as "if even death," but it is usually better to translate as "nothing but death will separate" or "only death will divide us."[53] In some languages, however, it is impossible to speak of death as the agent of an activity such as separating or dividing. In fact, in many languages there is no noun for death, only the verb "to die." Hence, this last clause may be translated as "if I leave you except when I die" or "if I leave you; only when I die will I leave you."

1.18   When Naomi saw that Ruth was determined to go with her, she said nothing more.

The Hebrew text has only pronouns to identify Naomi and Ruth. However, in most languages it is essential to indicate specifically that Naomi saw, and it is often useful to indicate that Ruth is the subject of was determined.[54]

She said nothing more is a rendering of the Hebrew expression "she ceased to talk to her." This does not mean that she refused to talk to her any more, but simply that she ceased to urge her to return to Moab (see NAB).

> [19]They went on until they came to Bethlehem. When they arrived, the whole town got excited, and the women said, "Is this really Naomi?"
>
> [20]"Don't call me Naomi, the Happy One," she answered. "Call me Mara,[a] the Sad One, because Almighty God has treated me very harshly. [21]When I left here I had plenty, but the Lord has brought me back without a thing. Why call me the Happy One when the Lord Almighty has condemned me and sent me trouble?"
>
> [22]This then, was how Naomi came back from Moab with Ruth, her Moabite daughter-in-law. They arrived in Bethlehem at the beginning of the barley harvest.
>
> ---
>
> [a] **Mara:** This means "bitter," which is here represented by *the Sad One* and *harshly*.

These verses introduce the third phase of Naomi's return to Bethlehem with Ruth. They involve a particularly effective way in which the emphasis upon Naomi's "emptiness" can be brought out.

1.19   They went on until they came to Bethlehem. When they arrived, the whole town got excited, and the women said, "Is this really Naomi?"

The whole town is really a figure of speech in which the designation of the whole stands for a part. That is to say, one speaks of "the whole town" when in reality one means only a large part of the inhabitants of the town. More particularly, in this case, the whole town means the women of Bethlehem. Something of the effect of this figure of speech may be realized in a translation such as "all the women of the town got excited and said."

Got excited is a good translation of the Hebrew term which may be rendered as "to be beside oneself."[55]

The verb said may not be a satisfactory term to introduce the following question. Accordingly, one may say "asked one another."

Is this Naomi, though in the form of a question, may have the value of an exclamation.[56] It is certain that the question of the women should not be understood to mean that they were uncertain who Naomi was; rather, they were surprised that she was in such a condition, without either husband or sons. In some languages, therefore, a more appropriate equivalent may be: "they exclaimed, It is Naomi!"

1.20   "Don't call me Naomi, the Happy One," she answered. "Call me Mara, the Sad One, because Almighty God has treated me very harshly.

The Hebrew text does not attempt to identify the meanings of Naomi and Mara, since to any Hebrew reader the meaning would be obvious: Naomi would be understood as meaning "happy" and Mara would be understood as meaning "bitter." However, it may be useful to follow the system employed in the TEV at this point by introducing something of the meaning of Naomi and Mara into the text itself: "Don't call me Naomi, the Happy One,... Call me Mara, the Sad One." One can, of course, simply keep the names Naomi and Mara and then provide the meanings for these terms in a marginal note. Observe that the TEV further explains Mara by a marginal note at this point.

Almighty God renders the Hebrew proper name Shaddai. It is impossible here to deal with all of the problems represented by this proper name. It occurs in a number of writings as another name for Yahweh,[57] and a translator may transcribe Shaddai as do some modern translations (for example, Bible de Jérusalem and Dhorme). A more common practice is to employ a translation such as "the Almighty" or "Almighty God." To do so implies, of course, that the name is translatable, whereas in reality its meaning is quite obscure.[58] However, the translation "Almighty" does have a very old tradition, and therefore one may be justified in using some such expression as "the most powerful God," "God who can do all things," or "the most powerful One."

Has treated me very harshly involves a pun in Hebrew, since Mara may be used not only to describe a person, but to identify the way in which one has been caused to suffer. Moffatt attempts to bring a play on words in his English translation: "Call me Mara, for the Almighty has cruelly marred me."[59] Sometimes one can preserve something of the pun by translating: "Call me Mara because the Almighty God has treated me bitterly," in which case it is necessary to have a footnote indicating that Mara means "bitter." There is, however, a serious complication for such a translation in English. If one says, "Call me Mara, the Bitter One," then "bitter" may be understood in a wrong sense, and even the phrase "has treated me bitterly" could appear to refer to God's attitude rather than to the extent of Naomi's suffering. Even a translation such as "it is a bitter lot that the Almighty has sent me," though somewhat more acceptable in English, would rarely be translatable literally into another language.

1.21   When I left here I had plenty, but the Lord has brought me back without a thing. Why call me the Happy One when the Lord Almighty has condemned me and sent me trouble?"

This verse makes quite explicit the theme of "emptiness," but it may be difficult to translate into some languages. Rarely can one talk about "having plenty" without indicating what is involved: things, family, relatives, prestige, etc. Sometimes one can translate: "When I left I had much, but the Lord has brought me back having nothing." One may in some instances employ the contrast between "being rich" and "now being poor." In other cases metaphorical expressions may be employed, for example, "When I left, my hands were full, but the Lord has brought me back with my hands empty."

The rhetorical question at the end of verse 21 may be more effectively rendered in some languages as a strong negative, for example, "Do not call me the Happy One." The Hebrew text at this point has "Naomi," but it may be preferable to use the meaning of the name rather than the name itself, since this is the way in which the speaker (Naomi) here uses it.

In the Hebrew text Lord is the subject of condemned me and "Shaddai" is the subject of sent me trouble. If a translation follows the Hebrew text literally, it may give the impression that the Lord and the Almighty are two different persons. In reality, the second clause is only a parallel expression used to intensify the meaning of the first clause. Accordingly, the TEV combines Lord and Almighty and makes them the single subject of the two verbs.

The verb translated condemned represents a Hebrew term which may be translated as "testified against me." The RSV at this point follows versional evidence in using a reading which means "afflicted." However, there seems to be a clear evidence that the Hebrew text should be followed at this point (see NEB and NAB).[60] A translation such as "has testified against me" or even "has condemned me" presupposes a certain guilt on the part of Naomi, but this is not made clear in the text. If the terms employed in a receptor language are too specific in this connection, it may be wise to use a more general expression, for example, "the Lord has turned against me."

Sent me trouble may be rendered in some languages as "caused me to suffer."

<u>1.22</u>   This then, was how Naomi came back from Moab with Ruth, her
Moabite daughter-in-law. They arrived in Bethlehem at the beginning
of the barley harvest.

This final verse of chapter 1 constitutes a summary paragraph. It adds no
new information except to introduce "the barley harvest," and this serves as a
kind of transition to what Ruth is described as doing in chapter 2.

The verbal construction in Hebrew makes it quite clear that verse 22 is to
be taken simply as a conclusion.[61] Accordingly, in the receptor language one
can employ a similar device to mark a concluding statement, for example, "this
is how it happened," "this then was how," "as a result," or even "so." The occurrence of the term <u>Moabite</u> is redundant; that is to say, the same information
has been given earlier. However, the repetition may be for emphasis, and thus
many translators may wish to retain the attributive, not only here, but also in
2.2, 21; 4.5, 10.

In many languages there is no precise equivalent for <u>barley</u>. In such cases
it is useful to employ a general word for grain. When such a general term does
not exist, one can sometimes employ a phrase which suggests similarity to
grains which are known in the region, for example, "millet-like grain" or "rice-
like grain."

Likewise, there may be no specific term for <u>harvest</u>, but this can be described as "the time when the barley grain was cut" or "the season when the
barley grain was brought to the barn."

CHAPTER 2

Ruth in the Field of Boaz

2 Naomi had a relative named Boaz, a rich and influential man who belonged to her husband Elimelech's family. ²Ruth said to Naomi, "Let me go to the fields to gather the grain that the harvest workers leave. I will find someone who will let me work behind him."

Naomi answered, "Go ahead, daughter."

³So Ruth went out to the fields and walked behind the workers, picking up the heads of grain they left. She happened to go to a field that belonged to Boaz, Elimelech's relative.

These opening paragraphs of chapter 2 consist of an introductory statement (vv. 1-2) as well as an introductory transitional statement (v. 3), which serve to introduce the principal account of the chapter (vv. 4-17). In a sense verse 3 belongs with what follows, since it speaks about Ruth's gathering the grain in the fields of Boaz. At the same time, it reiterates information which is contained in verse 1, that Boaz was a relative of Elimelech. Thus verse 3 plays a double role in the discourse structure.

The last episode of chapter 2 consists of verses 17-23. This includes a summary of what has happened, since it provides a setting in which Ruth tells Naomi the events of the day. It also reinforces the important fact that Ruth gleaned in the field of Boaz.

Throughout chapter 2 there are a number of rapid changes in the participants in the dialogue. First there are Ruth and Naomi, then Boaz and a servant, followed by a conversation between Boaz and Ruth, then between Boaz and his men, and finally a dialogue between Naomi and Ruth. A clear indication of these differences is indispensable for a proper understanding of the chapter.

The contents of chapter 2 do not focus primarily upon important events, but upon the feelings of the participants and the human relationships which are involved. Accordingly, they provide important insights into the emotional aspects of the story: the compassion of Boaz (v. 9), the surprise and humility of Ruth (v. 10), her joy and gratitude (v. 13), and the surprise and blessing of Naomi (v. 19).

The title Ruth in the Field of Boaz may seem to be unsatisfactory in some languages because it is often necessary to specify the relation between an agent such as Ruth and a place such as the field. Therefore one may require a title such as "Ruth Gleans in the Field of Boaz," "Ruth Works in the Field of Boaz," or "Ruth Gathers up Grain in the Field of Boaz." For a discussion of the translation of the verb "to glean," see the comments under verse 2.

2.1   Naomi had a relative named Boaz, a rich and influential man who belonged to her husband Elimelech's family.

Verse 1 is essentially an introductory statement anticipating information which would seem to belong in verse 3. In fact, some translators would prefer to place this information in verse 3, where it seems more logical. However, there is value in having the contents of verse 1 at the very beginning of the chapter, because the role of Boaz is so important to the rest of the story and because the mention of Boaz as being a rich and influential man emphasizes so significantly the theme of restoration, which is central to the whole story.[1] It is also important that the theme of restoration and "filling" be brought about by the event of harvest, which, in a sense, is a kind of celebration of the fertility of the earth and therefore an implied abundance.

The term relative is literally in the Hebrew text "acquaintance," but the text was understood by the Masoretes as "a kinsman," and this interpretation is preferable. It is not always easy to obtain a satisfactory term for relative, since it must designate a person who is related to one by some kind of blood tie but who is not a member of the immediate family. In this instance, of course, the blood relation is with the husband Elimelech, not with Naomi. In some languages the closest equivalent is "cousin." In other languages the equivalent is "brother," using a term which may designate all blood relatives in the same generation. On the other hand, a number of languages would simply say that Boaz belonged to "the same clan as Elimelech."

A rich and influential man translates what is literally in Hebrew "a mighty man of valor," but this expression involves two different components: (1) importance or prominence (see NAB) and (2) "wealth" (see NEB "well-to-do man"). In this particular context, the expression probably designates a particular social class of wealthy landlords[2] (see Moffatt, "a man of large property"). One could use in this context a phrase such as "a wealthy landlord" or "a rich and important man." In some societies the equivalent is "a wealthy elder," in which "elder" would emphasize cultural prominence rather than age.

Who belonged to her husband Elimelech's family may be rendered in a number of languages as "who belonged to the clan of Elimelech, the husband of Naomi" or "who was a part of the extended family of Elimelech, the husband of Naomi." In some languages it is essential to indicate the fact that Elimelech is now dead, for example, "the past husband of Naomi" or "the deceased husband of Naomi."

In dealing with terms for a clan, family, and tribe in Hebrew, there is a certain flexibility in meaning, but this is not the result of loose popular language.[3] We simply do not understand precisely the range of the distinctions in ancient Hebrew, and therefore the meanings seem at times to be somewhat fluid. In general, a term for "family" tends to designate the larger family, and a term for "clan" may be almost synonymous with "tribe."

The name Boaz sounds in Hebrew something like "in him is power." Other derivations have also been proposed, but there is certainly no evident derivation,[4] nor is there any indication that the meaning of the name Boaz has special relevance for the development of this story.

2.2   Ruth said to Naomi, "Let me go to the fields to gather the grain that the harvest workers leave. I will find someone who will let me work behind him."

Naomi answered, "Go ahead, daughter."

In this short dialogue between Ruth and Naomi, the first verb in the Hebrew text introduces a desire on the part of Ruth, and it is followed by a particle which is roughly equivalent to English "please." Naomi's answer is in the form of an imperative which expresses permission.[5] In many receptor languages the most natural equivalents would be "May I go to the fields to glean...?" and "Yes, go, my daughter." Since there is a question followed by a response, it is often useful to have for the first verb of speaking a term such as "ask" or "request," for example, "Ruth asked Naomi," followed by a term such as "answer" or "reply," for example, "Naomi responded."

The name Ruth at the beginning of verse 2 is followed immediately by the emphasis upon her being a Moabite, so that literally the text reads "Ruth the Moabitess." However, it is by no means always necessary to repeat this identification,[6] though perhaps in the Hebrew text the repetition does have emphasis and may be a none too subtle way by which the author keeps reminding the reader of Ruth's foreign background. (See comment on 1.22.)

In a number of languages there may be no technical term for "gleaning," which means gathering up the heads of grain which the harvest workers left behind by accident. In many societies such a practice is simply not economically profitable, while in other parts of the world such grain is left on the ground for animals to eat. It is, of course, always possible to describe gleaning as "gathering up the heads of grain which were left behind by the harvest workers," and it may be useful, therefore, to refer to certain Old Testament passages in which gleaning is mentioned (Leviticus 19.9-10; 23.22; Deuteronomy 24.19-22). It may even be useful to introduce a footnote, for example, "According to the law of the Hebrews, strangers, widows, orphans, and other poor people had the right to collect the ears of grain which had fallen from the hands of the reapers and were left behind in the field."

That the harvest workers leave states explicitly what is implied in the Hebrew text. However, the harvest workers may require some explanation in certain languages, possibly a descriptive phrase which will more precisely designate what these people were doing, for example, "those who were cutting the grain," "those who were harvesting the grain," or "those who were gathering in the grain from the fields."

Someone who will let me work behind him is literally in Hebrew "after him in whose eyes I shall find favor." This involves a rather frequent Hebrew idiom which occurs again in verses 10 and 13—though in the latter instance it is used primarily to indicate gratitude. In verse 2, however, it primarily involves permission, and it is translated in the NEB as "behind anyone who will grant me that favour."

Go ahead is an idiomatic way of saying in English "Proceed to do what you have suggested." In some languages this may be translated as "Go and do it" or "Do that."

The phrase my daughter, as has been noted in other instances, may need to be translated as "my daughter-in-law."

2.3   So Ruth went out to the fields and walked behind the workers, picking up the heads of grain they left. She happened to go to a field that belonged to Boaz, Elimelech's relative.

Since verse 3 begins with the result of what was anticipated in the dialogue between Ruth and Naomi, it is appropriate to introduce it by some such particle as so. In other languages the equivalent may be "therefore," "as a result," or "and so then."

It may be important in some languages to specify more clearly the kind of fields, for example, "fields of grain" or "fields where grain was being cut" (the equivalent of "harvest fields").

The workers in this context would in some languages be "the harvesters," "the men cutting the grain," or "the men gathering the grain."

Gathering heads of grain may be ambiguous in some languages since it might seem to imply that Ruth was likewise harvesting. Therefore it may be necessary to repeat what has already been said in verse 2, namely, "picking up heads of grain which had been left."

Verse 3 is to some extent repetitious of what has already been included in verses 1 and 2. This fact was already sensed by some ancient translators.[7] It is also possible to understand the first part of verse 3 as a conclusion to verse 2, while the second part of the verse could be the introduction to the section beginning with verse 4. On the other hand, the two parts of verse 3 can be closely combined as in the NAB: "The field she entered to glean after the harvesters happened to be the section belonging to Boaz of the clan of Elimelech."[8]

She happened to go translates what is in Hebrew more or less literally "her chance lighted upon a field." This Hebrew construction occurs elsewhere only in Ecclesiastes 2.14-15, in a context where the noun is normally rendered as "fate." It is, however, questionable whether any distinction can be made between "chance" and "fate" in the Hebrew.[9]

The context of the Book of Ruth would seem to indicate clearly that people are not in a position to change the course of history and, therefore, that it is really not by chance that Ruth arrives at the field of Boaz. It is evidently the action of Yahweh himself which determines such "happenings." As a result, most modern English versions use some such expressions as "happened" (RSV, NEB, NAB), but in a sense this may be said not to do full justice to the Hebrew text. On the other hand, it would be out of keeping with the context to emphasize too explicitly the aspect of "chance." Moffatt has in this context "it was her fortune to come upon," and one might very well translate as "she was fortunate to come upon." It would not be appropriate merely to translate: "she had the good luck to go to the field."

[4]Some time later, Boaz himself arrived from Bethlehem. "The Lord be with you!" he said to the workers.

"The Lord bless you!" they answered.

[5]Boaz asked his foreman, "Who is that young woman?"

[6]The man answered, "She is the foreign girl who came back with Naomi from Moab. [7]She asked me to let her follow the workers and

gather grain. She has been working from early morning until now, when she stopped to rest for a while under the shelter."

⁸Then Boaz said to Ruth, "Let me give you some advice. Don't gather grain anywhere except in this field. Stay here and work with the women. ⁹Watch them to see where they are reaping grain, and stay with them. I have ordered my men not to bother you. And whenever you are thirsty, go and drink from the water jars that they have filled."

¹⁰Ruth bowed down, with her face touching the ground, and said to Boaz, "Why should you be so concerned about me? Why should you be so kind to a foreigner?"

¹¹Boaz answered, "I have been told of everything that you have done for your mother-in-law since your husband died. I know how you left your father and mother and your own country, and how you came to live among a people you had never known before. ¹²May the Lord reward you for what you have done. May you have a full reward from the Lord God of Israel, to whom you have come for protection!"

¹³Ruth answered, "You are very kind to me, sir. You have given me courage by speaking gently to me, even though I am not the equal of one of your own servants."

These paragraphs constitute the first section of the central part of this story, which goes through verse 17. The heart of this account is the dialogue between Boaz and Ruth, and it well exemplifies the theme of restoration and "filling," since it is the assurance of Boaz to Ruth that she will be welcome to glean in his field and drink from the water jars which his servants have filled. Ruth's statement in verse 10 reiterates the theme of her being a foreigner, while the blessing which Boaz invokes for her in verse 12 reemphasizes "full reward." The theme of restoration and reward is further demonstrated in Boaz's invitation to Ruth to participate in the meal and the gift of food which he made. Also, his instruction to his servants to leave plenty of grain for her makes possible her rather large gleaning for the day, emphasized in verse 17.

2.4   Some time later, Boaz himself arrived from Bethlehem. "The Lord be with you!" he said to the workers.
"The Lord bless you!" they answered.

In Hebrew verse 4 begins with an adverbial expression often translated "behold." This is primarily a device to call special attention to the following expression, which in this case is the name of Boaz. However, in other languages a term denoting "behold" or "note" or "look" is often not appropriate. In English an equivalent expression might be "and there was Boaz coming" (NEB).

The verb arrived translates a perfect tense form in Hebrew, which suggests that the arrival of Boaz took place several hours after the events described in verse 3. This suggestion is confirmed by the statement in verse 7, which indicates that Ruth had already worked for some time in the field. Because of the lapse of time between verses 3 and 4, the TEV introduces a temporal transition at the beginning of verse 4, some time later. This could also be expressed as "Then after several hours Boaz himself came."

The expressions the Lord be with you and the Lord bless you are conventional formulas of greetings still current in some related Semitic languages.[10]

The Hebrew verb translated "bless" sometimes has the meaning of "greet," as in 1 Samuel 13.10 and 2 Samuel 13.25 (a parting salutation). The expressions the Lord be with you and the Lord bless you have a strictly liturgical value in present-day language, and they may seem quite strange in receptor languages as expressions of greeting. Some translators feel that it may be useful to introduce at this point typical indigenous greetings and responses—Boaz might say, for example, to the harvesters, "Did you work well?" or even "How are you today?"—but this type of cultural adaptation fails to provide the religious setting to the greetings which is so important to this context. The fact that these expressions are greetings can, of course, be identified by the verb chosen to introduce them, for example, "Boaz greeted the workers by saying, The Lord be with you, and the workers responded by greeting him in turn, The Lord bless you."[11]

It seems perfectly appropriate to us to say in English the Lord be with you, but in some languages this is quite impossible, both semantically and grammatically; one cannot make this kind of command in the third person. It is possible, however, in some languages to employ an expression of direct discourse, for example, "I ask the Lord to be with you" or "I pray to the Lord that he will be with you." Simply having the Lord "with a person" may not imply any special relationship, and therefore in some languages one must say: "I pray that the Lord will help you" or "I ask that the Lord be good to you."

Similarly, in the translation of The Lord bless you, it may be necessary for the workers to respond: "We pray that the Lord will be good to you" or "We ask that the Lord will show you favor." The choice of an appropriate term for bless is particularly difficult in some languages, since there may be at least three different terms which render the English expression "bless": (1) the blessing of a superior to an inferior (for example, "do good to" or "show favor to"); (2) the blessing of an inferior to a superior (for example, "praise"); and (3) a request for God to bless some object or person.

The position of expressions introducing direct discourse (in this case, the blessing formulas) must be determined by what is natural in the receptor language. More often than not, expressions introducing direct discourse (even such formulas as blessing and greetings) must occur before the direct discourse, rather than after it as in the TEV.

2.5   Boaz asked his foreman, "Who is that young woman?"

In Hebrew the term translated asked is simply "said," but since a question follows, most languages require an introductory verb of speaking which indicates the kind of direct discourse, namely, a question.

His foreman translates a Hebrew phrase: "his servant who had been appointed over the reapers." This expression may be translated in some languages as "the head man of his reapers," "the chief of his reapers," or "the man who commanded his reapers." The NAB has "the overseer of his harvesters," and Moffatt has "the foreman of the reapers in his service." His foreman may be translated as "the servant who worked for him" or "the servant who worked for

Boaz," and "his workers" may be "those who worked for him." In other languages, however, a possessive case of reapers may be required.[12]

Who is that young woman? is an attempt to focus properly upon the age of Ruth rather than to render literally "girl" as in some translations (NAB, NEB). There is no doubt about the emphasis upon her youth in the Hebrew reference to Ruth. At the same time, Ruth had been married, and her general appearance would certainly have merited the designation of "young woman."

Some translators may wish to employ some such question as "Who is this girl?" but this is really not sufficient for translating the Hebrew text, since the emphasis here is upon Ruth's relationship to some family or person. One may, therefore, employ a question such as "To which family does this young woman belong?" or "To which people does this young woman belong?"[13]

2.6   The man answered, "She is the foreign girl who came back with Naomi from Moab.

In the Hebrew text the man is specifically identified as "the servant who was in charge of the reapers," but in view of this context it is often not necessary to repeat what has already been said in verse 5. Therefore, one may translate as The man answered or "He replied."[14]

The expression the foreign girl...from Moab is in Hebrew literally "a Moabite maiden." In certain receptor languages, however, it may be important in this context to emphasize that the designation "Moabite" implies that she is "a foreigner." Therefore, this is made explicit in the TEV. The use of the definite article the with foreign girl seems fully justified (it is not without textual support[15]) in view of the fact that there had been so much interest in the return of Naomi and Ruth to the town of Bethlehem, as recorded in 1.19.

For the expression who came back with Naomi, see the comments on 1.10.

2.7   She asked me to let her follow the workers and gather grain. She has been working from early morning until now, when she stopped to rest for a while under the shelter."

She asked is literally in Hebrew "she said," but since what follows is a request, a verb such as "asked," "asked permission to," or "inquired whether she could" is fitting.

It is appropriate to use at this point either direct or indirect discourse in introducing what Ruth requested, for example, "She asked whether she could follow the workers," "She asked if she might glean" (NEB), or "She asked, May I gather up the grain left by the workers?" Whether direct or indirect discourse should be employed depends upon what is natural in the receptor language. Note that an expression of direct discourse would involve discourse within discourse, since it is quoting what Ruth said within a quotation of what the servant was saying to Boaz.

Gather grain translates what is literally in the Hebrew text "glean and gather among the sheaves after the reapers." This is the form employed by a majority of modern versions, but it represents a serious textual difficulty. Perhaps "among the sheaves" was mistakenly introduced into this verse from verse 15. According to verse 2, Ruth did not ask permission to gather among the sheaves; that would have been contrary to customary practice. Anyone who was gleaning was required to stay behind the reapers; that is to say, they could only gather after the harvesters had completed their work and in areas where the sheaves had been taken away.[16] Furthermore, it was only afterward (v. 15) that Ruth got permission to glean among the sheaves, which was an unusual favor. For these reasons the translator is encouraged to omit the prepositional phrase "among the sheaves" and to translate as in the TEV: follow the workers and gather grain. This type of translation has considerable support from ancient versions, but one cannot decide whether the early translations represented an older Hebrew original or whether they corrected the Hebrew text in a similar manner. There are a number of other suggestions for change which have been proposed, but none of these is fully acceptable.[17] Where necessary one can add a footnote introducing the literal form of the Hebrew text.

There are a number of textual problems of verse 7, but they have little bearing upon the problems of interpretation.

According to the accentual system of the Hebrew text,[18] the temporal phrase "from early morning until now" goes with the second part of this second sentence in verse 7. Hence the meaning: "from daybreak until now she hardly rested a moment." Therefore, one can translate: "So she came and remained here. From daybreak until now she has hardly rested a moment." The emphasis in this context is not upon "remaining," but rather upon the fact that Ruth continued working and thus did not rest from daybreak until the time of this conversation between Boaz and the servant.

In some languages it may be necessary to specify what kind of work was involved, for example, "she has worked gathering up the grain" or even "she has been diligent gathering up the grain."

The shelter in this type of context would probably be a temporary one made of upright poles and roofed with leafy branches or straw. Such a shelter is quite common in many parts of the world. If one wants to retain the rather difficult Hebrew expression "the house," a term which refers to a semipermanent structure should be used, rather than a term which indicates a house built of stone or some other more permanent structure.

2.8-9   Then Boaz said to Ruth, "Let me give you some advice. Don't gather grain anywhere except in this field. Stay here and work with the women. (9) Watch them to see where they are reaping grain, and stay with them. I have ordered my men not to bother you. And whenever you are thirsty, go and drink from the water jars that they have filled."

Since there is a shift in participants in direct discourse, it is important to introduce this change by some such transitional particle as then. This signals a short break in time and therefore also a break in the sequence.

The statement of Boaz to Ruth begins in Hebrew with a negative question which expects an affirmative answer: "Do you not listen?" The translator may very well follow the example of the TEV and use an affirmative statement instead of the question: Let me give you some advice.[19] The verb "listen" often has in Hebrew the meaning of "to understand." Therefore one may translate Boaz's introductory remarks as "you surely understand." However, in a number of languages "listen" often includes the component of understanding, as in Hebrew. In such cases, "listen" may be a very appropriate rendering.

The Hebrew text adds an expression meaning "my daughter" after "Do you not listen?" In many receptor languages it is entirely proper for a man to speak to a woman as "my daughter," especially if she belongs to a younger generation. At the same time it would be quite wrong to imply by such a form of address that Boaz was an old man.[20] In some languages, of course, a literal translation of "my daughter" would be entirely misleading, since the reader would assume that Boaz was actually addressing his own daughter or was a member of the same endogamous group. In such a case, the marriage of Boaz and Ruth would not have been possible. What is required here is an appropriate term of address which would indicate a marked degree of sympathy and kindness, while avoiding any specific reference to a close relative or any suggestion of courtship.[21] In some languages one may have an equivalent in "my little woman" or "dear lady."

However, in languages where no appropriate equivalent exists, it may be better to follow the example of the TEV and omit any term of address.

Don't gather grain anywhere except in this field represents a Hebrew expression which involves two negative verbs: "Do not go...and do not leave." A more natural order in most languages is "Do not leave this field in order to go and glean in another," but the two concepts may be combined in an emphatic form as in the TEV: Don't gather grain anywhere except.... One may also say: "Do not go anywhere else to gather grain."

Work with the women is literally in Hebrew "keep close to" or "cleave to." This is an emphasis upon "working close together with,"[22] since the women servants were the ones who normally gleaned in the fields after the menservants, who did the cutting.

The admonition at the beginning of verse 9 translated watch in the TEV may be rendered more or less literally in Hebrew as "let your eyes be upon (the field)" or "keep your eyes on (the field)." This is an expression which means "watch (the field)" or "pay attention to (the field)." In reality this means to pay attention to what is going on in the field and may refer specifically to Ruth's activity, namely, "to search."[23] If there is a specific reference to "the field," then it may be necessary to say "this field" or "this my field."[24]

In the Hebrew text it is quite clear that the subject of reaping is "the menservants," that is, the harvesters. Ruth is admonished to follow the "women servants" and to stay with them. The entire first sentence of verse 9 may be rendered as "Watch where the men are reaping, and follow the women servants who are gleaning" (cf. NEB).

The statement I have ordered my men not to bother you is in Hebrew a question marked with a negative particle, but implying an affirmative answer. Therefore it can appropriately be translated as a statement. Most translators employ a perfect tense: I have ordered my men or "I have given them orders." The Hebrew perfect tense expresses an action which is apparently accomplished at the very moment of the utterance—at least there is no indication of any prior statement by Boaz to the workers—so that in some languages one may translate correctly with the present tense: "Now I give orders to...."[25]

To bother you is literally "to touch you," but in this context it means "to harm" or "to trouble."

The Hebrew term translated water jars in the TEV means any kind of vessel or utensil, but obviously in this context the reference is to jars containing water.

Go and drink from the water jars that they have filled is literally in Hebrew "go to the vessels and drink what the young men have drawn." These two expressions may be conveniently coalesced, as in the TEV. In some languages it may be necessary to specify they as "my men" or "the menservants," and it may also be necessary to specify in this context "water." This has been made explicit in some of the ancient versions.[26]

2.10   Ruth bowed down, with her face touching the ground, and said to Boaz, "Why should you be so concerned about me? Why should you be so kind to a foreigner?"

The TEV rendering Ruth bowed down, with her face touching the ground represents a Hebrew expression which is often rendered literally: "She fell on her face, bowing to the ground." The two expressions ("fell...bowing...") represent a measure of redundancy, and this is sometimes reduced in some of the early versions.[27] It is rare that one can translate literally "she fell on her face," since this tends to be understood as being accidental rather than intentional. Some translators employ a phrase such as "to cast oneself down," but this again is a rather strange rendering, since it seems to imply some kind of violent activity rather than simply homage and gratitude. Accordingly, the TEV employs the expression bowed down, with her face touching the ground. In some languages it may even be necessary to translate: "bowed very low, touching her forehead to the ground," since in many receptor cultures this is the equivalent expression.

Said to Boaz must be rendered in some languages as "asked Boaz," "inquired of Boaz," since what follows is a question.

Be so kind to translates what is in Hebrew literally "found favor in your eyes" (see comments on verse 2). The emphasis here is upon the favor which Boaz had shown to Ruth and thus "to be kind to" is appropriate. It is also possible to combine "kindness" with "taking notice of," and so to translate: "Why are you so kind as to take notice of me?"

In the Hebrew expression translated often as "take notice of me when I am a foreigner," there is a pun on the roots of the verb and the noun.[28] Some translators try to introduce a play on words in a corresponding English translation such as "to deal with me as a friend though I am a foreigner," though in this instance there is very little resemblance between the sounds.[29] It is always nice to be able to reproduce a play on words in a source language, but it is only rarely that one can do so with success. Attempts to reproduce a play on words frequently result in a rather artificial kind of expression.

A foreigner may be rendered in some languages as "someone not from this country," "a person from a different tribe," or "someone from a distant country" (or "another country"). In this context "distant" is purely a relative matter, but it is often used as a means of designating a foreigner.

The statement by Ruth that she is a foreigner is important in the development of the story. This prepares the ground for Boaz's statement beginning in verse 11.[30]

2.11-12   Boaz answered, "I have been told of everything that you have done for your mother-in-law since your husband died. I know how you left your father and mother and your own country, and how you came to live among a people you had never known before. (12) May the Lord reward you for what you have done. May you have a full reward from the Lord God of Israel, to whom you have come for protection!"

These verses form an important unit, even though the structure of verse 11 is normal prose, whereas verse 12 has a type of poetic structure. It consists of two lines with the meter 3 + 3 ; 3 + 2 + 2, with the following units: // The Lord recompense you for what you have done / and a full reward be given to you // by the Lord the God of Israel / under whose wings / you have come to take refuge //. If one can conveniently reproduce in translation something of the poetic structure of verse 12, this is fine; but it is seldom that one can do justice to such a short poetic portion embedded within what is essentially a prose structure.

The passive expression I have been told of everything may be rendered in some languages as "people have told me about" or "I have heard about."

Your own country represents a Hebrew expression which may be rendered as "land of your kindred" or "land of your birth." It occurs only three times in the patriarchal stories (Genesis 11.28; 24.7; 31.13). In some languages an equivalent is "the place where you were born" or "the land of your tribe." Even a translation such as "your tribe" may be employed.[31]

In some languages it may be necessary to employ two verbs for left, since the action of leaving one's father and mother may be quite different from that of leaving one's own country. In the first instance one may need to say: "You left behind your father and mother," and in the second instance: "you departed from your own country."

A people you had never known before is in some languages "a new people" or "a people that you were not acquainted with previously." It is important to avoid the implication that Ruth had never known about such people. It is the act of experiencing which is important in this context. Therefore, in some languages one must translate "among a people that you have never before had any dealings with" or "among a people with whom you have never lived before."

In some languages verse 12 may require considerable restructuring. This has already been done in one of the ancient versions: "The Lord, the God of Israel, reward your deed; he, under whose wings you have come for refuge, give you a full reward."[32] But in many languages it is difficult to use this type of third-person request; therefore one must often have some introductory expression such as "pray," "entreat," or "request," for example, "I pray that the Lord will reward you."

In a number of languages reward is equivalent to "pay you in exchange," "give you a prize for," or "compensate you in exchange for," for example, "I pray that the Lord will pay you back for all that you have done," "...give you a gift...," or "...show a special favor...." In this context it is important to note that it must be a positive benefit or gift and not some kind of punishment, which would often be the interpretation of the expression "pay you back for what you have done."

To whom you have come for protection is literally in Hebrew "under whose wings you have come to take refuge." It is not clear to what kind of imagery the "wings" belong. One normally thinks of the wings of a bird, but some commentators believe that this is a reference to the wings of the cherubim,[33] or even the wings of the winged sun-disk.[34] It is even possible that the interpretation of wings of a bird and wings of the cherubim were both associated with this Hebrew phrase from a very early time, so that the two images in a sense reinforced each other.[35] The use of a verb meaning "to cover" or "to seek shelter" does, of course, suggest the imagery of the bird.[36] Some persons, however, have proposed to change the imagery completely and to render the Hebrew word not as "wings" but as "skirts."[37] Though this is a possible translation, it is a highly improbable one.[38] The basis for the comparison is made quite clear in the phrase "to take refuge." Because of this, it is sometimes possible to retain the expression "under whose wings," because one can state precisely what this figure of speech implies, for example, "may the Lord give you a full reward, since you have come to him to seek shelter as under the wings of a bird."

Though the retention of the figure of speech "under his wings" is very desirable, it is sometimes very difficult to understand, particularly in this kind of very short poetic structure. For that reason the TEV employs to whom you have come for protection.

2.13   Ruth answered, "You are very kind to me, sir. You have given me courage by speaking gently to me, even though I am not the equal of one of your own servants."

Again, the answer which Ruth gives in verse 13 represents a type of poetic structure. The verse consists of three lines with the following meter: 3 + 2, 2 + 2, 3 + 2; and the literal translation of these units may be given as // You are most gracious to me, my lord / for you have comforted me // and spoken kindly to / your maidservant // though I am not / one of your maidservants //. Though it would certainly be interesting to be able to reproduce something of the poetic structure of verse 13, rarely can one do so. Not only is the passage very short,

but it does not have the type of content (elaborate figures of speech and conden-
sation of information) which is typical of most poetry.

You are very kind to me may be rendered in some languages as "you are
very good to me," but in Hebrew this is literally "I have found favor in your
eyes." (See comments on verse 10.) Though this Hebrew expression does seem
rather elaborate, it is essentially no different in meaning from a modern English
expression, "Thank you, sir."39 The translators of the NEB apparently felt that
Ruth's expression of thanks is sufficiently expressed in the remaining part of
the verse, and therefore they employed for this first expression merely "Indeed,
sir."

Some translators feel that the imperfect tense of the Hebrew verb "to find"
must refer to some future event or must express a subjunctive mood, but this
seems far from being necessary.40

What is rendered as sir in the TEV is in Hebrew literally "my lord" or
"my master." It is, however, merely a conventional term of respectful address,
and the translator should employ the equivalent form in the receptor language.
In some instances this will mean the use of an appropriate honorific or a form
of address indicative of the difference in status between Ruth and Boaz. There
may be certain complications in languages which employ the same word for
"master" or "sir" and for "Yahweh." These complications have been dealt with
elsewhere.41

The phrase speaking gently represents what in Hebrew is literally "have
spoken to the heart of your servant." In Hebrew the use of the third person,
"your servant," emphasizes the respect which Ruth shows for Boaz. In modern
English it is much better to use the first person, by speaking gently to me.

Speaking gently may be rendered in some languages as "speaking kindly to,"
"speaking with good words to," or even, idiomatically, as "speaking with smiling
eyes" or "speaking with a soft face."

Even though I am not the equal of one of your own servants is literally in
Hebrew "though I am not like one of your servants." This expression makes perfectly good sense, and there seems to be no reason why one should follow some
of the ancient versions which employ different textual bases.42 To emphasize
that this is an expression of Ruth's humbleness, the TEV translates: the equal
of.

> 14At mealtime Boaz said to Ruth, "Come and have a piece of bread,
> and dip it in the wine sauce." So she sat with the workers, and Boaz
> passed some roasted grain to her. She ate until she was satisfied, and
> she still had some food left over. 15After she had left to go and gather
> grain, Boaz ordered the workers, "Let her gather grain even where the
> bundles are lying, and don't bother her. 16Pull out some heads of grain
> from the bundles and leave them for her to pick up. And don't reprimand
> her."
> 17So Ruth gathered grain in the field until evening, and when she had
> beaten it out, she had nearly fifty pounds. 18She took her grain, went back
> into town, and showed her mother-in-law how much she had gathered.
> She also gave her the food left over from the meal. 19Naomi asked her,

"Where did you gather grain today? Whose field have you been working in? May God bless the man who took notice of you!"

So Ruth told Naomi that she had been working in the field of a man named Boaz.

²⁰Naomi said to her, "May he be blessed by the Lord, who always keeps his promises to the living and the dead." And she went on, "That man is a close relative of ours, one of those responsible for taking care of us."

²¹Then Ruth said, "Besides everything else, he told me to keep gathering grain with his workers until they finish the harvest."

²²Naomi said to Ruth, "Yes, daughter, you might be molested if you went to another man's field. It will be better for you to work with the women in Boaz's field." ²³So Ruth worked with them, and gathered grain until all the barley and wheat had been harvested. And she continued to live with her mother-in-law.

These paragraphs of chapter 2 include two principal sections: (1) verses 14-17 complete what took place in the field, and (2) verse 18 begins a summary in which Ruth tells her mother-in-law what has happened during the day. In some languages it may be proper to have a paragraph break beginning with verse 18, but other translations besides the TEV have a paragraph break beginning with verse 17, since this forms a summary for what has preceded and at the same time introduces indirectly the following episode.

2.14   At mealtime Boaz said to Ruth, "Come and have a piece of bread, and dip it in the wine sauce." So she sat with the workers, and Boaz passed some roasted grain to her. She ate until she was satisfied, and she still had some food left over.

At mealtime is the temporal setting for the event of speaking; this is in full accord with the syntactic division of the Hebrew text, though it is different from what is found in one of the ancient versions.[43] In some languages, however, one cannot employ a phrase such as "at mealtime." Rather, a clause is needed, such as "when it was time to eat" or "when the people began to eat."

For the term bread, see the comments on 1.6. This is essentially a term with generic meaning, often translatable as "food." In some instances it may be better to translate it as "have something to eat."

It is important to indicate in an expression such as have a piece of bread that this is something which Boaz is giving to Ruth. He is not commanding her to eat her own food, but rather is offering her something. This may be expressed in some languages as "let me give you a piece of bread," "I want to give you a piece of bread," or "take this piece of bread."

Wine sauce represents a Hebrew expression which is often translated merely as "wine," but the substance seems to have been a kind of vinegar (see Moffatt) which was a by-product of wine-making.[44] The substance appears to have served as essentially a kind of sauce,[45] and in some translations one may have "a sauce consisting of sour wine." In English the most satisfactory equivalent seems to be simply wine sauce. In some languages one may employ "sour wine as a kind of sauce" or "wine used as a sauce." In practically all languages there is some expression for sauce, since the use of some type of liquid into which food is placed or which is used to improve or modify the taste of food is widespread.

In this context the expression the workers is literally "the reapers," but this is not restricted to the male servants. It is better, therefore, to employ a general expression such as the workers (TEV), rather than place Ruth exclusively with the male servants or segregate her with the female servants. Such a separation would likewise be inappropriate in view of the fact that Boaz passed the roasted grain to Ruth, who evidently was not sitting far from him.

The verb translated passed, referring to Boaz's act of giving roasted grain to Ruth, occurs only at this point in the Old Testament, and its meaning is uncertain. Even in late Hebrew the verb is very rare and used only in contexts describing that part of a vessel or jar which one touches in handling it.[46] Translators of ancient versions did not understand the meaning of this Hebrew verb, and they read into it another Hebrew verb meaning "to heap up."[47] This reading is also found in some modern translations[48] and is defended by some commentators who argue that the meaning of "to pass" would be incorrect in speaking of what Boaz did.[49] However, the meaning of "to heap up" should not be employed. There is just a slight possibility that the verb had reference to some particular process in the preparation of the grain,[50] but since there is no certainty with regard to the meaning of the term, the rendering of "to pass" seems to be the most satisfactory, at least until new evidence as to its meaning is found.

Roasted grain is a very common food in the Middle East[51] and is greatly appreciated in many other parts of the world. There should therefore be no difficulty in finding an appropriate equivalent.

Until she was satisfied should not be translated in such a way as to imply that she was in any way gluttonous; what is important is to indicate that Boaz was sufficiently generous to her to make her feel satisfied and happy. Until she was satisfied is often rendered "until she had had enough," "until she felt good," "until she had all she wanted," or "until she was no longer hungry."

2.15-16   After she had left to go and gather grain, Boaz ordered the workers, "Let her gather grain even where the bundles are lying, and don't bother her. (16) Pull out some heads of grain from the bundles and leave them for her to pick up. And don't reprimand her."

The TEV rightly translates after she had left to go and gather grain. A translation "when she got up..." can be misleading, for it might imply that at this very time Boaz ordered his servants to treat her with special consideration, thus suggesting that Ruth was still present when Boaz gave the order to his servants. This, of course, was not the case, and therefore it may be well to translate the first clause as "when Ruth had gotten up to go gather grain" or "after Ruth had gone to gather grain." One may also employ an independent sentence as a translation of this initial clause: "Ruth went off to glean," followed by "then Boaz ordered his servants."

The workers is literally in Hebrew "his young men," but there is no special emphasis upon the age of Boaz's workers, and therefore it is better to use some such expression as "his men" or "his servants."

Ordered is literally in Hebrew "ordered, saying." The use of two verbs for speaking is typical of Hebrew, but it is not at all necessary to reproduce both in a receptor language.

The direct discourse Boaz ordered his servants: "Let her..." may be changed to indirect discourse if that seems more natural in a receptor language, for example, "Boaz ordered his servants to let her gather grain...."

Let her gather grain renders a verbal form in Hebrew which expresses a possibility,52 but in most languages this is appropriately indicated as permission: "Let her glean," "If she wants to, she may glean," or "Do not stop her from gleaning." For comments on the expression where the bundles are lying (often translated literally as "among the sheaves"), see the comments on verse 7. In ancient times a reaper would grasp a handful of stalks with one hand and cut it with a sickle held in the other hand. The handfuls were left on the ground, and the women would gather them and bind them into bundles, technically called "sheaves." These were stood upright on the ground for drying or curing.53 Later they might be brought to the threshing floor where the grain would be separated by having it beaten out or stamped out by cattle.

Normally, the persons gleaning in a field would pick up only the heads of grain which were left behind by those who carried the sheaves to the barn or threshing floor. In this instance Ruth was given the special privilege of gathering among the sheaves or bundles of grain, and thus she was able to pick up what would normally have been picked up by the women servants. In this context, therefore, it may be helpful to have a supplementary note explaining precisely what the procedures were in ancient times, and thus the significance of Ruth's receiving permission to gather grain even where the bundles were standing.

Don't bother her refers primarily to verbal rebuke. It is essentially the same type of expression which concludes verse 16. One may render this expression as "don't tell her not to do so," "don't scold her," or "don't speak angrily to her."

Pull out some heads of grain from the bundles states explicitly what the reapers were instructed to do in order to provide Ruth with more grain than she would normally be able to pick up. The "bundle" in this instance would refer to the stalk the harvester held in his left hand when he would cut with a sickle. Usually, only what would fall to the ground by chance would be available for those who were gleaning, but in this instance the harvesters get instructions to drop some of the stalks intentionally and leave them for Ruth. In order that this process may be perfectly clear, one may need to translate "pull out some of the heads of grain from the bundles which you have in your hand as you cut them, and leave some stalks for Ruth to pick up." The admonition to "pull out some heads of grain" is quite emphatic in the Hebrew form,54 and it can therefore be translated in some languages as "you shall by all means pull out...for her."

Leave them for her to pick up may need to be somewhat more explicit in some languages as "leave them for her to find and pick up." One should not imply that the reapers were to be careless in their work so that Ruth would have to pick up what they unintentionally left.

Don't reprimand her is another way of saying "do not scold her," "do not tell her not to do it," or even (if direct discourse is preferable) "do not say to her, Do not glean here."

2.17   So Ruth gathered grain in the field until evening, and when she had beaten it out, she had nearly fifty pounds.

As already noted, verse 17 concludes the account of Ruth's gathering grain in the field of Boaz. It begins with a particle translated so, which indicates result and which may be translated in some languages: "as a result," "and so at the end," or "and thus finally."

Until evening is most generally rendered "until the sun went down," "until the sun could be seen no longer," or "until the sun had disappeared."

The Hebrew verb translated beaten...out occurs elsewhere only in Judges 6.11, where it has this same literal meaning of threshing out small quantities of grain by knocking them loose from the stalk by means of a curved stick, club, or wooden hammer.[55] One ancient version makes the instrument explicit by translating: "she beat with a stick what she had gleaned."[56] Another translation makes explicit both the instrument and the two events of hitting the heads of wheat and driving out the grain: "she beat with a stick what she had gleaned and drove out the grains."[57] The latter translation is an excellent descriptive model for those languages which lack a technical term for "beating out." In some instances, however, one must use a causative expression, such as "cause to fall out" or "cause to become loose."

Though there is no indication of precisely where this threshing takes place, it no doubt was done in the field.[58] The Hebrew expression which is rendered in the TEV as nearly fifty pounds is literally "about an ephah of barley," but there is no certainty as to what this measurement implied. Some scholars believe that it was approximately 40 liters;[59] others agree that the ephah was approximately 40 liters during the Hellenistic period, but cannot say what it was earlier.[60] Archaeological findings may some day provide us with reliable information,[61] but with the data now available it is impossible to give an exact equivalent of the ephah of the time of Ruth. The translator, however, must employ something in his text, and there are three major possibilities: (1) he may simply transliterate the Hebrew measure, with or without some explanatory note; (2) he may employ a receptor language term which represents a measure more or less equivalent to the Hebrew term; or (3) he may use a combination of the source-language term as well as some receptor-language equivalent, as was done in one of the ancient versions.[62] In keeping with the first procedure, he would simply use "ephah" in the text (see NAB), with possibly a footnote or a symbol to show that it is explained in a table of weights and measures or glossary. In keeping with the second procedure, the translator could use a term such as "bushel" (see NEB, Moffatt). Following the third procedure, he would employ some such expression as "it was about an ephah, that is to say, a basketful of barley." In this case the term for "basket" would have to be a measure essentially equivalent to an ephah in the Hellenistic period, that is about 40 liters or 40 quarts. For many speakers of English the term "bushel" is a rarity and quantities of grain are more often described in terms of weight rather than bulk. For this reason the TEV uses the expression nearly fifty pounds. In some instances translators may simply employ a rendering which implied that the amount of grain was considerable: "a good measure of grain" or "a lot of grain." That would emphasize the fact that this was an abundant result for the day's work. Such a translation has interesting ancient support.[63]

2.18   She took her grain, went back into town, and showed her mother-in-law how much she had gathered. She also gave her the food left over from the meal.

Most modern translations begin a new paragraph with verse 17, as the TEV does, but some have a new paragraph begin at verse 18 (see JB). It is even possible to divide verse 18 and to take the first part as constituting a conclusion to the previous section. A new paragraph would then begin after the clause went back into town (see Moffatt). If this is done, it will be important to introduce the following clause with "Then Ruth showed to her mother-in-law how much she had gathered." A break in the structure at this point obviously requires more specific indication of who does what, and proper names must be used in place of pronouns, even as in some of the ancient versions.[64]

Showed her mother-in-law how much she had gathered is the reading of the Hebrew text in a few manuscripts, but all other manuscripts have "her mother-in-law saw what she had gleaned."[65] The difference in the two readings involves merely a different way in which the vowels of the Hebrew verb are understood. It is better, however, to follow in this instance the text employed in the TEV, since this produces a far smoother sequence of events. It avoids the suggestion that after Ruth took the grain back into the town, her mother-in-law discovered how much she had gleaned, with the implication that Ruth did not tell her exactly what she had done.

She also gave her the food renders what is literally in Hebrew: "she brought out and gave her." "Brought out" does not indicate the place from which she took the food. The term "cupboard" has been suggested,[66] but there is no indication whatsoever as to what place is involved. It would be possible to translate simply as "she also showed her mother-in-law the food that was left over from the meal."[67]

The last clause of the Hebrew text of verse 18 is literally "gave her what food she had left over after being satisfied." This is a reference to what has already been stated in verse 14. A literal rendering of the Hebrew text may, however, lead to misunderstanding, since it could imply in some languages that Ruth was inconsiderate of Naomi and therefore had only reserved for Naomi what she did not want. It is better, therefore, to translate as "gave her the remainder of the food," "gave her what she had left over from lunch" (NAB), or "gave her what she had saved from her meal" (NEB). The NEB employs a very useful device of placing the modifying clause concerning the food earlier in the verse and stating in the last clause merely "gave it to her."

2.19   Naomi asked her, "Where did you gather grain today? Whose field have you been working in? May God bless the man who took notice of you!"

        So Ruth told Naomi that she had been working in the field of a man named Boaz.

The questions in the Hebrew text of verse 19 would seem to be in a wrong order, since "Where did you glean today?" appears to be more specific than "Where did you work?" Some translators, therefore, feel justified in reversing the order. The second is really a double question, involving not only "going" but also "working."[68] This is made explicit in the NAB as "Where did you go to work?" In a sense the second question is also highly specific, for Naomi's intention was no doubt to find out the particular field in which Ruth had gleaned. Therefore, from the standpoint of the development of the text, the first question should be regarded as being more general and the second as more specific. For this reason the TEV renders the second question as Whose field have you been working in? That the second question focuses upon the owner of the field is indicated by the benediction which Naomi then expresses: May God bless the man who took notice of you!

The third person imperative in the expression may God bless the man who took notice of you is difficult to translate into a number of languages. In the Hebrew text the corresponding expression is literally "blessed be the man who took notice of you." This passive expression is often awkward to render, and a translation such as "blessings on the man" (NEB) is of very little help in finding a practical solution to translation in most receptor languages. It may, therefore, be necessary to employ, as in so many cases, some verb to introduce direct discourse, for example, "I pray that the Lord will bless the man." In this type of context, blessing implies "helping," "doing good to," or "looking with favor upon," and is the opposite of cursing. It should not be related merely to material prosperity (though this component of meaning was important in biblical Hebrew) and certainly should not be related to games of chance or gambling.[69]

For the expression took notice of you, see the comments on verse 10, where the same Hebrew verb is used.

The second part of verse 19 in the Hebrew text is somewhat confusing and misleading. Literally, it may be rendered as "so she told her mother-in-law with whom she had worked and said, The man's name with whom I worked today is Boaz." In the first place, it may be preferable to use proper names—Ruth told Naomi—rather than to say "she told her mother-in-law."

The clause "with whom she had worked" may be misleading because it might suggest that she worked together with Boaz. This, of course, was not the case; she simply worked in the field which belonged to Boaz. Furthermore, it is misleading to have, as in the Hebrew text, a repetition of the information with regard to working, first in an indirect form and then in a direct form. For this reason the two expressions are coalesced in the TEV to read: Ruth told Naomi that she had been working in the field of a man named Boaz. Some ancient translators recognized the problem in the discrepancy between questions and answer, and this led them to formulate what seemed to be a more satisfactory answer by Ruth.[70]

2.20 Naomi said to her, "May he be blessed by the Lord, who always keeps his promises to the living and the dead." And she went on, "That man is a close relative of ours, one of those responsible for taking care of us."

The verb translated said introduces an emphatic statement and in some languages may be appropriately translated as "Naomi exclaimed" (see NAB) or, as in some languages, "Naomi said strongly to her."

May he be blessed by the Lord involves a Hebrew construction which is literally "blessed be he with reference to the Lord," but the preposition refers clearly to the Lord as the author of the action.[71] Such a passive expression, however, is extremely difficult in many languages and therefore one must use an active form, for example, "May the Lord, who always keeps his promises to the living and the dead, bless him." In other instances it may be necessary to introduce this expression by a verb marking direct discourse, for example, "I pray that the Lord may bless...."

The clause who always keeps his promises to the living and the dead obviously refers to the Lord and not to Boaz. It is important that any ambiguity in the construction be avoided.[72]

The term translated promises is rendered in some translations as "kindness" (RSV) and in others as "mercy" (cf. NAB). The focus here, however, is upon "loyalty" (cf. NEB "keep faith with"). One may translate: "The Lord is always loyal to the living and to the dead" or "The Lord continues to be loyal to those who are living and to those who have died." In many languages, however, the expression of keeps his promises is a very effective rendering, since this clearly specifies the way in which God continues to be loyal. Keeps his promises may be rendered as "does what he has promised he will do," "helps them even as he said he would help them," or "is good to them just like he said he would always be good to them."

And she went on may be translated as "and she also said to Ruth" or "and in addition she said."

In some languages that man must be rendered as "Boaz," since it is a specific reference and therefore the proper name (which has already been mentioned in verse 19) must be employed.

A close relative of ours is rendered in a number of different ways in different receptor languages, for example, "this man is one of our brothers," "this man belongs to our clan," "this man is like one of our family," or "this man is one of our large family" (in which "large family" is a reference to the extended family in contrast with the immediate family).

The Hebrew term translated one of those responsible for taking care of us

is a highly technical one which could be literally translated as "one of our re-
deemers" or "one of those who has the right of redemption over us."[73] Such a
person was a relative who was obliged to protect the interests of the family and
clan. This involved the individual's freedom, his goods, and his posterity. One
of the duties of such a "redeemer" was to produce an heir to one who had died.
Another obligation involved buying property that was in danger of being lost to
the family by being sold outside the family group. As is clear in chapter 4, both
of these duties play an important role in the story of Ruth, and the same term
occurs in 3.9-12 and 4.1,3,6,8,14. Various aspects of the duties involved will
be pointed out in the comments on these verses.[74]

In most receptor languages it is necessary to employ some type of descriptive phrase which will identify not only the relationship of a person to a particular
family or clan, but also something of his obligations. Accordingly, the TEV employs the translation a close relative of ours, one of those responsible for taking
care of us. An equivalent descriptive phrase might also be "he is one of those
who can help us as a relative" or "he is one of those who can provide for us as
one does for members of a family." Where levirate marriage is well known in a
society and where there are other similar responsibilities and obligations involved, one may even employ a translation such as "he is one of those who can
take us as widows." Such an expression could be classified as a fully dynamic
equivalent and one which would be in keeping with this context.

In some languages, however, it is not easy to speak of "responsibility."
One of those responsible for taking care of us may need to be rendered as "one
of those who must take care of us," "one of those who our customs say must take
care of us," or "one who must take care of us because he is related to us."

2.21   Then Ruth said, "Besides everything else, he told me to keep
gathering grain with his workers until they finish the harvest."

In the Hebrew text the name Ruth is immediately followed by the expression "the Moabitess," but it is not always necessary to repeat this expression
(see the comments on 1.22 and 2.2). In a number of ancient versions also the
repetition was regarded as being superfluous.[75] Some of the ancient versions do
introduce, however, the person spoken to in this case, namely, her mother-in-
law: "Ruth said to her mother-in-law."[76]

Since Ruth here provides information which she has not already communicated, it may be necessary to change the verb said to something such as "added"
(NAB). It is not clear whether the information that Ruth provides in verse 21 is
directly related to her recognizing that Boaz has certain responsibilities for her
and Naomi, but it is certainly not out of keeping with what has been stated in the
latter part of verse 20. Some commentators suggest this relation,[77] and it is
hinted at in some translations (cf. Moffatt "'Yes,' said Ruth..."). It is questionable, however, whether one is justified in trying to introduce this type of
connection between verses 20 and 21.

Besides everything else, he told me is a free rendering of a complex Hebrew construction which may be literally rendered as "there is still this, which

he said."[78] Direct discourse within direct discourse may present certain problems in some receptor languages. Therefore, a second direct discourse can often be changed into an indirect one: "he told me to stay close" (NEB) or <u>he told me to keep gathering grain with his workers</u> (TEV).

To keep gathering grain with his workers reflects a Hebrew expression containing the phrase "keep close to." (See the comments on verse 8.)

The term <u>workers</u> has in Hebrew the masculine form, but the emphasis is not here upon the sex of the servants; it is rather a more general term to include both male and female servants. The focus is upon "working with his servants," that is, in his field rather than in the field of some other man. A number of ancient versions, however, used the feminine form of the noun for "servants" (namely, "women servants"[79]), but that is a secondary reading introduced to harmonize this information with what occurs in verses 8, 22, and 23 of this chapter.

<u>Until they finish the harvest</u> involves both the barley and the wheat harvest. Normally the wheat harvest took place about a month later than the barley harvest. Traditionally the wheat harvest ended at the Feast of Weeks, seven weeks after the barley harvest had begun.[80]

2.22   Naomi said to Ruth, "Yes, daughter, you might be molested if you went to another man's field. It will be better for you to work with the women in Boaz's field."

The Hebrew text has "Ruth her daughter-in-law," but it is not necessary to reproduce "daughter-in-law" in this context since the relationship is quite clear (cf. NEB, NAB).

In some languages a general verb for <u>said</u> is appropriate in introducing Naomi's comment in this verse. In other languages the link between verse 22 and verse 21 needs to be made more evident, and therefore one may use a verb such as "rejoined" (NAB), "responded," or "replied in turn."

For the translation of <u>daughter</u>, see the comments on verses 8 and 9. The connotation of this term is one of affection and kinship. A modern English equivalent may be "my dear" (see NAB).

The Hebrew text of verse 22 has a different order from what occurs in the TEV. The comparative <u>it will be better for you to work with the women in Boaz's field</u> actually precedes the statement concerning Ruth's possibly being molested if she goes to another man's field. It seems more natural in English, however, to state the reason first and then the result or conclusion, namely, that Ruth had better stay with the servants of Boaz. For this reason the TEV reverses the order.

The clause <u>it will be better for you to work with the women in Boaz's field</u> is in Hebrew a comparative construction, but the second part of the comparison is left out.[81] This makes the Hebrew clause correspond more or less to the English construction "you had better accompany his girls" (Moffatt). However, in some receptor languages it may not be possible to leave out the second member of a comparison. One may have to say, for example, "it is better for you to stay with his servants than to go with the servants of some other man." Perhaps a more natural expression for this comparison would employ a statement containing an expression of necessity, for example, "you should only accompany his women servants" or "you must stay with his servants."

You might be molested translates a Hebrew verb which often means merely "to meet." In this context, however, it means "to meet with hostility." There seems no reason for following the NEB "let no one catch you," since the meaning seems clearly to be "molest," "insult," or "harm." One may even have the active verbal construction: "so that no one may attack you in the fields" or "so that the reapers in the field of someone else may not attack you there."

2.23   So Ruth worked with them, and gathered grain until all the barley and wheat had been harvested. And she continued to live with her mother-in-law.

Verse 23 serves as a summary of the contents of chapter 2, but it seems to provide no clue as to further developments in the story. Yet there is a suggestion for the transition which occurs in the following verse, the first verse of chapter 3. Chapter 2 ends with Ruth living with her mother-in-law, but the first verse of chapter 3 contains Naomi's declaration that she should seek a home for Ruth, since a permanent arrangement for Ruth would obviously be more satisfactory than continuing indefinitely with her mother-in-law. Thus, though the text of verse 23 does not seem to provide a clue as to the rest of the story, in fact it actually does. It is the issue of a permanent home and relationship which is regarded as so essential for Ruth.

It is important to recognize that verse 23 is a type of summary, and therefore a particle such as so is quite appropriate. This may be rendered as "and therefore," "and as a result," or "in keeping with this."

It would be wrong to translate the first clause of verse 23, Ruth worked with them, in such a way as to give the impression that Ruth was hired by Boaz as one of his servants. Rather, she continued to gather grain or to glean on the same basis as Boaz had specified to his servants in verse 16. It is rather misleading to follow the RSV translation, "she kept close to the maidens of Boaz," since this could imply quite a different dimension of relationship.

Until all the barley and wheat had been harvested can be restructured as "till the harvesters had cut and brought in all the barley and wheat," which is somewhat more specific.

In some of the ancient versions, the final clause, and she continued to live with her mother-in-law, is placed at the beginning of chapter 3,[82] but there seems to be no special need to follow this division.[83] It may be useful, however, to introduce the last clause with an expression such as "after that" (that is to say, "after the work in the field"). One is not advised to follow the alternative Hebrew reading, "and she returned to her mother-in-law." This reading has very little textual support and seems clearly secondary, since it appears to be only a smoother transition from the first statement to the second.[84]

CHAPTER 3

Ruth Finds a Husband

3 Then Naomi said to Ruth, "I must find a husband for you, so that you will have a home of your own. [2]Remember that this man Boaz, whose women you have been working with, is our relative. Now listen. This evening he will be threshing the barley. [3]So wash yourself, put on some perfume, and get dressed in your best clothes. Then go where he is threshing, but don't let him know you are there until he has finished eating and drinking. [4]When he lies down, notice the place. After he goes to sleep, go, lift the cover, and lie down beside him. He will tell you what to do."

[5]Ruth answered, "I will do everything you say."

These opening paragraphs of chapter 3, which introduce the climax of the story contained in the paragraphs which follow, are skillfully organized. First, there is a reference to the need for finding a husband for Ruth, which serves to relate chapter 3 to what has immediately preceded in chapter 2. Second, there is a continued reference to Boaz, who has become the key figure in the plot. Finally, certain events recorded in the following paragraphs are anticipated by means of the advice which Naomi gives to Ruth. Furthermore, Naomi's instructions stop just short of the crucial point, namely, the reaction of Boaz when he discovers Ruth lying at his feet. All of this provides the reader with insight into the role of Naomi and heightens the reader's interest in the outcome.

The title Ruth Finds a Husband is one way to describe the focus and content of chapter 3. But a literal translation of this English expression can be quite misleading in some languages. One might understand such a phrase as meaning that Ruth accidentally came across a husband or that she went out looking for a husband (as one would look for a lost coin) and found him. In some languages an equivalent might be "Ruth Gets a Husband" or "A Marriage Is Arranged for Ruth" (suggesting the initiative of Naomi). It is, of course, possible to employ a somewhat more specific section heading, for example, "Boaz Promises to Help Ruth" or "Boaz Promises to Take Responsibility for Ruth," but too specific a title might serve to tell too much of the story. Some translators have suggested such headings as "Ruth Goes to Meet Boaz" or "Naomi Sends Ruth to See Boaz," but one may argue that the real significance of this chapter is not so much Ruth's actions as Boaz's response.

3.1   Then Naomi said to Ruth, "I must find a husband for you, so that you will have a home of your own.

This first verse forms a transition with the last verse of chapter 2, since it takes up the matter of Ruth's need for having security and a home of her own rather than living with her mother-in-law. But this verse is not merely transitional; it establishes the theme of the rest of the book, namely, a husband and a home for Ruth.

The adverbial conjunction then should not be understood as "immediately" or "right then," but as a reference to the next significant element in the sequence of events.[1] The lapse of time could not have been more than a few weeks at most, for the threshing of the barley had not been completed, even though both the barley and the wheat had been harvested. The harvest included cutting the stalks in the field, gathering and tying them into sheaves, and transporting the sheaves to the threshing floor.

After a paragraph break and section heading, it is important to introduce the participants in the dialogue; therefore the introductory statement should read: Naomi said to Ruth.

The sentence I must find a husband for you, so that you will have a home is in Hebrew literally "Should I not seek a home for you, that it may be well with you?" (On the use of the question in Hebrew, see the comments on 2.8.) In the verbal form of the Hebrew text an aspect of obligation is implicit, and for this reason one should translate: "I must find" or "I must arrange."[2]

A literal translation of the clause I must find a husband for you can easily be misunderstood, since it might imply that Naomi would actually go out and search for a husband for Ruth. Such a translation becomes especially misleading if for find one employs the same word as may be used in the receptor language in speaking of a young man going out to find (or to court) a wife. In many languages, therefore, find a husband for you must be expressed as a causative, for example, "I must cause you to have a husband." In other languages one can employ a more or less technical term, for example, "I must arrange a marriage for you."

Both here and in 1.9 the Hebrew terms for home indicate a condition of rest and security attained through marriage.[3] In general it is necessary to make explicit the basis for this rest and security, though in some modern English translations the basis is left implicit, for example, "I want to see you happily settled" (NEB; cf. also Moffatt). The TEV text, however, makes the basis for this happiness and security quite explicit, I must find a husband for you. There are other ways in which this can be expressed, for example, "I want to see you married," "I want to be sure you have a husband," or "I want you to be married so that you will be happy and secure." (Cf. Smith-Goodspeed and JB.[4])

In some languages there is no such term as home. Rather, one must specify a relation between husband and wife, for example, "I must cause you to get married so that you will have someone to live with" or "I must arrange for some man to marry you so that you will live happily." It is usually not enough to employ a term which simply designates a house, such as "so that you may have a house." As noted in 1.9, a widow would live in a house, but this would not imply having a home.

3.2   Remember that this man Boaz, whose women you have been working with, is our relative. Now listen. This evening he will be threshing the barley.

The first sentence of verse 2 in Hebrew is "Now is not Boaz our kinsman, with whose servants you were?" The negative question marker indicates clearly that an affirmative answer is expected, so a translator is fully justified in turning this question into an emphatic affirmative statement. This may be done in several ways, for example, "Now there is our kinsman Boaz; you were with his girls" (NEB) or "Now here is our kinsman Boaz, with whose girls you have been working" (Moffatt).

The phrase Boaz...is our relative contains old information which has to be remembered. So a translation Remember that... is certainly accurate. One of the difficulties with the verb "remember" is that it may imply that someone is to remember what has been forgotten. This is not the implication of Naomi's statement to Ruth. What she really means is "Bear in mind that" or "You must be aware that." One may also translate: "As you know, Boaz is one of our relatives."

The Hebrew text does not specify working, but it is a perfectly normal addition. The TEV rendering whose women you have been working with seems considerably more natural than the literal rendering "with whose women servants you were."

For the interpretation of our relative (literally "one of our relatives"), see the comments on 2.1. The Hebrew noun is slightly different from the one used in 2.1, but there is no evidence that the difference in form implies a significant difference in meaning.[5] It is therefore best to take the two forms as being synonymous.

Now listen is an idiomatic way of translating into English a Hebrew adverb traditionally rendered as "see" or "behold" (see RSV and Smith-Goodspeed). Most modern versions (e.g. NAB, NEB, and Moffatt) simply omit the adverb, but there is a value in trying to reproduce something of the significance of this Hebrew expression, since it does serve to call attention to what immediately follows. Some languages have special particles which mean "pay attention now," "mark this," or "hear."

The TEV rendering this evening he will be threshing the barley is in Hebrew literally "he will be winnowing the threshing floor of barley." This means "he will be winnowing the barley which has been threshed on the threshing floor." Winnowing actually followed the threshing, which was the process of separating the grain from the straw by beating it with flails or having animals trample it. The straw was then lifted with wooden forks, leaving the grain mixed with chaff and dust on the floor. Winnowing consisted of throwing these into the west wind by means of a wooden shovel. The heavier grains would fall back on the threshing floor, while the wind would carry away the dust and the chaff.[6] In Palestine the west wind normally begins to blow about two o'clock in the afternoon and continues through the evening and into the night. It is important that the wind be not too strong or blustery, and this may explain why the evening was regarded as the best time for winnowing.[7] Probably Boaz himself did not do the winnowing, but simply supervised his servants as they did the work. Perhaps Boaz stayed at the threshing floor during the night in order to guard it against thieves.

One of the reasons why the TEV does not specify "winnowing" is that such a process is rarely known or understood at the present time by English-speaking people. Furthermore, winnowing would be regarded as only part of the process of threshing, and therefore the TEV uses the more general term at this point. However, where winnowing is known, a specific term for this process should be employed, and it may be useful in some instances to add a marginal note to explain this process. Where a technical term for winnowing is lacking, it is sometimes possible to use a descriptive phrase such as "he will be shaking out the dirt from the barley,"[8] "he will be separating the grain from the chaff," or "he will be separating the grain from the leaves."

3.3   So wash yourself, put on some perfume, and get dressed in your best clothes. Then go where he is threshing, but don't let him know you are there until he has finished eating and drinking.

Wash yourself should be understood in the sense of "to bathe" (NAB).

Put on some perfume represents a Hebrew expression normally translated as "to anoint."[9] One of the difficulties involved in using a word meaning "to anoint" is that this is a very generalized expression in Hebrew and would not necessarily be understood in this context to mean "anoint with good-smelling oils." Therefore, it seems better to be somewhat more specific than the Hebrew text and to translate "put on some perfume," since this was certainly the meaning of Naomi's instruction to Ruth.

The rendering get dressed in your best clothes is a very satisfactory idiomatic equivalent of the Hebrew expression. However, it is true that most Hebrew manuscripts[10] have at this point a singular noun, and one may therefore appropriately translate "put on your best cloak." This may very well refer to a large piece of cloth worn as an outer garment, but this is not the mantle or cloak mentioned in verse 15 which Ruth used to carry home the relatively large quantity of barley.

Rather than merely go where he is threshing, the Hebrew specifies "go down to the threshing floor." This would imply that the threshing floor was situated at a point lower than the town of Bethlehem, but there is no specific information as to its location.[11] Where languages do employ rather precise indications of movement, such as "going up" or "going down," one should attempt to follow the Hebrew usage, but the indication of elevation in this context is by no means crucial or particularly significant.

What is rendered in the TEV as don't let him know you are there represents a Hebrew expression which may be translated literally as "do not make yourself known to the man" (RSV). The obvious meaning here is "do not let yourself be recognized by him."[12] The Hebrew expression must be restructured in a number of languages, for example, "do not let your presence be known to the man," "don't let him recognize that you are there," or "don't let him know who you are." Even some ancient translators recognized the need for restructuring and translated the Hebrew expression as "do not show yourself to him."[13]

In this context drinking refers to the drinking of wine or some other alcoholic beverage. In some languages the process of eating and drinking is represented by a single verb.

3.4   When he lies down, notice the place. After he goes to sleep, go, lift
           the cover, and lie down beside him. He will tell you what to do."

Lift the cover renders what is in Hebrew literally "uncover the place of his
feet." The meaning of what Ruth did was essentially to ask for Boaz's protection.[14] Of course, the idea of a marriage proposal may very well have been implicit in the act,[15] but there is no clear evidence that this expression is a euphemism for sexual intercourse, as has been suggested by some scholars.[16] On the
other hand, the Hebrew terms translated "uncover," "feet," and "lie down" are
often associated with sexual acts, and therefore the expression lends itself to
this type of interpretation.[17] Even some ancient translators tried in several
ways to weaken or alter the meaning.[18]

Since it is altogether possible that what Ruth did may be misunderstood in
a receptor culture, it is appropriate to have some marginal note at this point indicating that what Ruth did was a symbolic way of asking for protection. In fact,
in some translations the meaning of the act is incorporated into the text itself,
for example, "lift up the cover at his feet to ask for his protection." This may
be done on the basis that the act itself was a recognized symbol for asking for
security.

3.5   Ruth answered, "I will do everything you say."

The Hebrew text has simply "and she said...." However, in view of the
fact that there is a change in the one who is speaking, it is often better to make
the subject (Ruth) explicit: "Ruth answered" or "Ruth responded" (see NAB,
NEB, TEV).

In a number of Hebrew manuscripts and in various versions, the pronoun
"me" is added.[19] Hence, the statement of Ruth may be rendered as "I will do
everything you have told me" or "...whatever you tell me" (NEB).

> [6]So Ruth went to the threshing place and did just what her mother-in-law
> had told her. [7]When Boaz had finished eating and drinking, he was in a
> good mood. He went to the pile of barley and lay down to sleep. Ruth
> slipped over quietly, lifted the cover and lay down beside him. [8]During the
> night he woke up suddenly, turned over, and was surprised to find a
> woman lying there. [9]"Who are you?" he asked.
> "It's Ruth, sir," she answered. "Because you are a close relative, you
> have the responsibility of taking care of me. So please marry me."
> [10]The Lord bless you," he said. "You are showing even greater family
> loyalty in what you are doing now than in what you did for your mother-
> in-law. You haven't looked for a young man, rich or poor. [11]Now don't
> worry, Ruth. Everyone in town knows that you are a good woman.
> I will do everything you ask. [12]It is true that I am a close relative, and
> am responsible for you, but there is a man who is a closer relative than
> I am. [13]Stay here the rest of the night, and in the morning we will find
> out whether he will be responsible for you. If so, well and good; if not,
> then I swear by the living God that I will take the responsibility. Now lie
> down and stay here till morning."
> [14]So she lay there beside him until morning, but she got up before it
> was light enough for her to be seen, because Boaz did not want anyone
> to know that she had been there. [15]Boaz said to her, "Take off your cloak

and spread it out here." She did, and he poured out almost a hundred pounds of barley, and helped her pick it up. Then she returned to town with it. [16]She went to her mother-in-law, who asked her, "How did you get along, daughter?"

This principal section of chapter 3 contains three major parts: (1) Verses 6-7 carry out what has already been indicated in the instructions of Naomi to Ruth in verses 3-4. (2) Verses 8-13 form the crucial part of the story with everything developing as one would expect, except for the revelation contained in verse 12, namely, that there is another person who is an even closer relative than Boaz. This, of course, forms the basis for the next principal episode in the story of Ruth, namely, the legal procedure in 4.1-12. However, this second section does conclude with assurances from Boaz to Ruth in verse 13. (3) The final part of this section, verses 14-16a, completes the time period and gives evidence of Boaz's intent in his generous gift of barley in verse 15. This would appear to be a significant element in Naomi's assurance to Ruth that Boaz will carry forward his purpose as quickly as possible.

3.6   So Ruth went to the threshing place and did just what her mother-in-law had told her.

What the TEV has rendered as went is in Hebrew more specifically "went down." See the comments on verse 3.

3.7   When Boaz had finished eating and drinking, he was in a good mood. He went to the pile of barley and lay down to sleep. Ruth slipped over quietly, lifted the cover and lay down beside him.

He was in a good mood renders what is literally in Hebrew "his heart was merry." In this context happiness is the result of good eating and drinking, a state of well-being, but there is nothing in the Hebrew expression that would suggest any excess. There are a number of ways in which the meaning of the Hebrew idiom may be expressed, for example, "he had a sense of well being" (Smith-Goodspeed), "he felt at peace with the world" (NEB), "he had a merry time" (Moffatt), "his heart was sweet," "his liver was happy," and "his eyes were bright," to suggest only a few ways in which happiness may be expressed in various receptor languages.

The location where Boaz lay down is not at all specific in Hebrew. It is therefore quite appropriate to translate by some such general expression as "by," "near to," or "at the edge of" (NAB). In this context a meaning such as "at the end of" (Smith-Goodspeed) or "at the far end of" would seem to be erroneous.

The Hebrew text only specifies a "pile" or "heap," but obviously this is a reference to a "heap of grain" (NEB, Moffatt), not a "straw stack." One cannot be certain whether the grain was threshed or not.[20] Usually one must specify what a pile or heap consists of; therefore one may say: the pile of barley or "the heap of grain."

The Hebrew text says simply "she came secretly," but it may be better in some languages to indicate the component of "secrecy" in the verb itself, for example, "she slipped over quietly," "she crept in noiselessly," or "she stole up to."

There was some lapse of time between Boaz's lying down to sleep and Ruth's lifting up the cover of his feet. In some receptor languages it may be necessary to specify this time lapse by suggesting the intervening implicit state, namely, "when he was asleep." The necessity for this was felt already by early translators.[21]

For the rendering of lifted the cover and lay down, see the comments on verse 4. At this point some ancient translators sometimes tried to "purify" the text.[22]

3.8   During the night he woke up suddenly, turned over, and was surprised to find a woman lying there.

During the night renders a Hebrew expression "and it was in the middle of the night," but this does not indicate precisely "at midnight" (RSV, Moffatt, Smith-Goodspeed). An expression such as "about midnight" (NEB) is a more correct equivalent. In a number of languages there are several different terms for periods of the night, each period having a specific name or designation. A translator should select a term for a time near midnight, without attempting to be too precise in the designation.

He woke up suddenly renders a Hebrew expression "the man started up." "The man" is Boaz, and one should employ either a definite pronoun "he" or the name "Boaz." The verb "started up" implies "to start up out of sleep"; therefore he woke up suddenly is a close natural equivalent. The Hebrew verb is intransitive (at least in its active voice), and accordingly it is difficult to justify taking "the man" as the object with some kind of indefinite and implied subject, as in the case of the NEB: "something disturbed the man as he slept."

Turned over is the rendering employed in most modern English versions, with the exception of Moffatt, who adapts the meaning of the verb to the context and thus renders "and bent forward." The meaning of this verb is not at all clear. There are only two other occurrences of the verb in the Old Testament: Judges 16.29, where it is used of Samson and his behavior in the temple of Dagon, rendered there "to grasp" (Samson grasped the two middle columns); and in Job 6.18, where it is generally translated "turns aside." In each instance the rendering of the verb depends largely on the context and on the meaning of related terms in cognate languages.[23] The interpretation "to turn over" is largely based on Arabic, in which a related verb means "to twist (oneself)."[24] This meaning, however, would imply that Ruth was lying by the side of Boaz rather than at his feet. In fact, one of the ancient versions seems to have interpreted the situation in this way by commenting that Boaz nevertheless controlled his desires and did not approach Ruth.[25] Other versions seemed to have missed the meaning of the Hebrew verb and take it as a synonym of the preceding verb, "to start up" or "to tremble."[26] In summary, one may say that the rendering given by Moffatt ("and bent forward") seems to be the best, since it appears to fit most precisely the context.

The phrase was surprised to find translates a vivid Hebrew expression, literally, "see, a woman lay at his feet." This kind of vivid style can be quite effectively reproduced in a number of languages. The interjection in the Hebrew text marks surprise.[27] The relation between the surprise and finding a woman lying at his feet must be expressed in a number of languages as cause and effect, for example, "he was very much surprised because he found a woman lying at his feet." The meaning of to find in this context is, of course, "to discover," and this is sometimes represented by a verb "to see," for example, "he was very much surprised because he saw a woman lying there at his feet."

The qualifying phrase lying there must sometimes be made a separate clause, for example, "he saw a woman; she was lying there at his feet."

3.9 "Who are you?" he asked.
   "It's Ruth, sir," she answered. "Because you are a close relative, you have the responsibility of taking care of me. So please marry me."

Expressions introducing direct discourse, such as he asked and she answered, normally precede the quoted words. In English, however, it is possible to place such expressions after direct discourse if the direct discourse is not too long, or they may be embedded within the direct discourse, as in the case of she answered in this verse. Some languages employ identifications both before and after direct discourse, thus providing an oral equivalent of quotation marks.

It's Ruth, sir translates a Hebrew phrase "I Ruth your servant." This phrase must often be rendered in a somewhat different form, for example, "I am your servant, Ruth" or "I am Ruth, your servant." This use of "servant" must not imply that Ruth is asking to be made a servant, nor does it mean that she has already accepted the status of a servant to Boaz. Rather, it is an oriental expression of politeness and indicates Ruth's attitude of respect for Boaz.[28] In other languages an expression of respect may take the form of a special title for Boaz, for example, "I am Ruth, your honor" or "you who are so important, I am just Ruth, a humble person."

In a number of languages it is more appropriate to translate "she responded" or "she replied" rather than she said, since Ruth was clearly responding to the question which Boaz had just asked.

The two sentences Because you are ... marry me translate a single Hebrew sentence which is literally "spread your skirt over your maidservant, for you are next of kin." This sentence has a poetic structure in Hebrew with a meter of 3 + 3. It is usually difficult to reproduce a very short section of poetic structure in a receptor language, especially one which involves a rather rare figure of speech, which, if translated literally, might very well lead to a wrong understanding of Ruth's intent.

For a discussion of the meaning of close relative, see the comments on 2.20. Because the relation between a close relative and marriage may not be at

[53]

all clear, the TEV makes explicit the significance of being a close relative, namely, having the responsibility of taking care of someone. This is necessary for those cultures in which such a responsibility is by no means automatically included in such a relation. In fact, in many languages an expression "close relative" would imply that marriage would be impossible, since marriage of close relatives would mean incest. This means that it may be necessary to use a term for close relative or "next of kin" which will indicate clearly that Boaz is not someone who would be traditionally prohibited from entering into marriage with Ruth. In some languages the appropriate expression is "close relative by marriage" or "close relative because of the one I was married to," a phrase which may be necessary in this context, but which, of course, must not be used throughout.

The consonants in the Hebrew expression rendered in the TEV as marry me may have two different meanings, depending upon the vowels which are associated with the consonants. With one set of vowel markings the meaning is "spread your skirt over your maidservant," and with the other set of vowel markings the meaning is "spread your wings over your maidservant." In this connection see the comments on 2.12. In general the meaning seems quite clearly to be a request for protection, with the specific meaning of marry me,[29] but most translators and commentators prefer to retain the literal idiom "spread your skirt over your maidservant."[30] In a sense, both components of meaning, union and protection, are present in the expression "spread your skirt over your maidservant,"[31] so that the difference in meaning between the two possible ways of writing the vowels with the Hebrew consonants is not great.

One of the serious difficulties involved in a literal translation of the Hebrew idiom, "spread your skirt over your maidservant," is that it is too easily interpreted as an invitation to sexual intercourse, and this seems to be out of keeping with the characters of the story. In most instances, therefore, it may be best to give the meaning of the idiom in the text, and, if necessary, provide a literal translation in a marginal note.

3.10   "The Lord bless you," he said. "You are showing even greater
        family loyalty in what you are doing now than in what you did for your
        mother-in-law. You haven't looked for a young man, rich or poor.

For the sentence The Lord bless you, see the comments on 2.20. At this point the TEV text changes a passive expression in Hebrew (literally "may you be blessed by the Lord") into an active form. A number of languages do not have this type of so-called optative expression, and hence some type of introductory expression of speaking or desiring may be required, for example, "I ask the Lord to bless you," "I pray that the Lord will bless you," or even "I am sure that the Lord will bless you." A translation such as in the NEB, "the Lord has blessed you," does not seem justified in view of the evident optative meaning of the Hebrew verbal form.[32]

In the Hebrew Boaz here addresses Ruth as "my daughter," but in some languages such words at this point would be inappropriate, since they would only confirm the suspicions that the reference to "close relative" did indeed imply an incestuous relation. The closest equivalent in some languages is "dear young lady" or "dear woman." It would seem particularly inappropriate in many languages for Boaz to address a woman who had already been married by a term such as "daughter." Therefore the TEV omits this address.

The second sentence of verse 10 in Hebrew is literally "you have made your last loyalty greater than the first." The references here would be perfectly clear to the ancient Hebrew reader, but they are certainly obscure to the average present-day reader of this story. The theme of the "first loyalty" was already spoken of by Boaz in 2.11, a reference to Ruth's concern for her mother-in-law and loyalty to her. The "last loyalty" is a reference to Ruth's preference for Boaz as a husband. This loyalty is stated more precisely by Boaz as You haven't looked for a young man. Since the reference to the "last loyalty" and the "first loyalty" are quite obscure to the average reader, it is usually preferable to follow the practice of the TEV in making the relation explicit: You are showing even greater family loyalty in what you are doing now than in what you did for your mother-in-law.

In the phrase translated looked for a young man, the Hebrew text employs an extremely rare use of the verb "go after" or "follow." In fact, the only similar context in the Old Testament is Proverbs 7.22, in which "the beloved one" is the goal of such an action. One might assume that a verb such as "run after" or looked for would be almost universally applicable to courtship and marriage, but this is not necessarily true. Some languages may require quite a different type of expression, for example, "to cause a young man to be interested in you," "to cause a young man to desire you," or "to cause a young man to see you as beautiful." On the other hand, some languages simply use "to want to marry a young man" or "to want to have a young man as a husband."

The phrase rich or poor reverses the Hebrew word order, "poor or rich." In many languages this reversed order seems far more natural. Even some early translators felt the necessity for a different order.[33] Rich or poor is a very elliptical expression, and it must be filled out in a number of languages, for example, "You have not run after a young man, if he were rich or if he were poor," "You have not run after either a rich young man or a poor young man," or "You have not run after young men, one who is rich or one who is poor."

3.11 Now don't worry, Ruth. Everyone in town knows that you are a good woman. I will do everything you ask.

The TEV is the only modern translation which restructures the order of the sentences of the source text. The Hebrew order is: (1) "don't be afraid"; (2) "I will do everything you ask"; (3) "all people know that you are a good woman." The object of Ruth's fear is not the possibility of Boaz's refusing help to her, but the possibility that the people of the town will oppose her because she is of Moabite origin.[34] In order to make this meaning quite clear, a change in the order of clauses seems essential. In fact, it may be appropriate to make the relation even more explicit than in the TEV. One may translate, for example:

"Dear woman, do not be afraid, for everyone in town knows that you are a good woman."

Everyone in town renders a Hebrew expression which is literally "the whole gate of my people." The gate is mentioned here as the center of the social life of the community. For its importance, see the comments on 4.1 and compare a parallel expression in 4.10. In this type of context "gate" refers to the city and "the whole gate" is a reference to the whole city in the sense of "all the people of the city" or "all of the citizens." This particular expression occurs only here in the Old Testament, but its meaning is quite certain. There seems no reason to think that this is a specific reference to some council of the people, as is suggested by the Smith-Goodspeed translation. It is rare that one can employ a term for "gate" in reference to a city, particularly since in most parts of the world cities no longer have gates. However, in certain ancient translations a term for gate has been retained with certain interesting possibilities of interpretation.[35]

In Hebrew the adjective good implies ability, efficiency, and moral worth. The NEB emphasizes the first aspect of meaning by translating "a capable woman," but most other translations prefer to indicate the factor of moral worth or value, for example, "a worthy woman," "a good woman," or "a fine woman."[36]

3.12   It is true that I am a close relative, and am responsible for you, but there is a man who is a closer relative than I am.

For the clause I am a close relative, and am responsible for you, see the comments on verse 9. In some languages, in order to say I am responsible for you, one must introduce some aspect of obligation as a separate component of the phrase, for example, "I must take care of you," "it is my duty to take care of you," or "our customs demand that I take care of you."

This reference to a closer relative introduces a factor of surprise into the story. Everything has proceeded as Naomi outlined it to Ruth, and no mention has been made until now of the other person who is an even closer relative. It is surprising that Naomi apparently did not know about the closer relative.[37] If she did know, she did not communicate the fact to Ruth, or at least the writer of the story does not indicate that she did. At any rate, Boaz knew, and it is this knowledge which prompted his rather cautious behavior. He was evidently attracted by Ruth, since otherwise he could have evasively referred her to the closer relative.[38] The closer relative obviously had prior claims and prior duties, and for Boaz to have disregarded the other man's rights might have resulted in serious consequences.[39]

In many languages it is difficult to speak of a closer relative. Sometimes one can say "one who is nearer to your family," "a man who is not as separated from your family as I am," or "one who stands closer to your mother-in-law than I do." In some languages it is even necessary to use some specific form of address, for example, "someone who can call your mother-in-law sister" or "someone who can call your mother-in-law aunt." This, of course, depends upon the generation which is involved, and since Ruth would presumably be marrying a person in her own generation, it may be preferable to have the closer relative be related to Naomi as nephew to aunt. In almost every society there are slight differences of usage in kinship terms, and therefore it is necessary to represent accurately the relationships which are specified within each language-culture system.

3.13   Stay here the rest of the night, and in the morning we will find out whether he will be responsible for you. If so, well and good; if not, then I swear by the living God that I will take the responsibility. Now lie down and stay here till morning."

Boaz's statement to Ruth that she should stay there the rest of the night would imply that he wanted to protect Ruth from the dangers of the night, possibly an encounter with thieves or men who were drunk at the harvest season. Threshing and winnowing were not women's work,[40] and Ruth's presence at the threshing floor could certainly lead to a misinterpretation of her motives. Had she been detected, people would have probably thought that she was present as a prostitute.

In the morning...I will take the responsibility is in Hebrew literally, "in the morning, if he will do for you the kinsman's part, well and good; but if he is not pleased to do for you the kinsman's part, then I will do for you the kinsman's part, as the Lord lives." Some restructuring of this Hebrew sentence is almost imperative if the results are to be clear and stylistically acceptable. For one thing, it is not always necessary to repeat "to do for you the kinsman's part." This is generally better translated as "be responsible for you" or "have the duty of helping you."

Part of the confusion and obscurity in Boaz's statement results from the fact that he anticipated some type of legal action, but this is not specifically stated. The TEV makes reference to this by translating in the morning we will find out. It might even be possible to employ "we will find out before the tribunal" or "we will find out when this case is judged."

It may seem rather strange that the closer relative is not specifically named. It is somewhat difficult always to refer clearly to that person without having a proper name with which to identify him. It is all the more necessary, therefore, that phrases such as "that man," "that person," or "that closer relative" be clearly marked.

For comments on the meaning of "to do the kinsman's part" see 2.20 and 3.9.

The idiomatic expression well and good (TEV, NEB) is quite close to the Hebrew phrase.[41] In other languages it may be necessary to use an expression such as "let him do so," "that will be fine," or "that is all that I can do."

Boaz's assurance to Ruth that he will help in every possible way is concluded by an oath. This may be introduced in a number of ways in different languages, for example, "I promise before God," "I make a strong promise, calling God to listen," "I promise, and God will remember," or "I promise, using God's name."

The Hebrew oath formula, literally, "on the life of the Lord," occurs frequently in the Old Testament.[42] For the ancient Jewish people an oath "on the life of the Lord" was the strongest possible statement of intent in which "he who swears puts the whole substance and strength of his soul into the words he speaks,"[43] since the oath was pronounced on the basis of God's strength and with him as a participant.[44]

In many languages, however, it would be quite meaningless to say "on the life of the Lord." One must often employ a somewhat different expression, for example, "I swear it by the Lord" (NEB). The NEB phrase, however, does not communicate the sense of "life," and for that reason the TEV employs a somewhat altered formula: I swear by the living God. In many languages it is quite impossible to speak of swearing by the life of someone. A more appropriate formula may be "I swear by the name of...." Therefore one could employ "I swear by the name of the living Lord." In English the phrase "living Lord" is not widely employed, but the phrase "living God" is relatively well-known and therefore seems appropriate for the TEV translation.

3.14   So she lay there beside him until morning, but she got up before
          it was light enough for her to be seen, because Boaz did not want any-
          one to know that she had been there.

Before it was light enough for her to be seen translates what in Hebrew is literally "before one could recognize another," but the basis for such recognition must be made explicit in most languages. Accordingly, the TEV employs a reference to light. One may, however, employ a negative expression, "when it was still so dark that no one would recognize her." The necessity for making the reason explicit was already felt by ancient translators.[45] In some languages there is a special term for designating early morning darkness, and therefore a reference to such a period of relative obscurity can be employed in this context.

Because Boaz did not want is in Hebrew "and he said." There is no doubt that Boaz is the subject which needs to be made explicit,[46] but no modern translation states clearly to whom the utterance is addressed. Failure to do this is probably due to the fact that there are three different possible interpretations: (1) Boaz may be addressing his servants;[47] (2) he may be addressing Ruth directly to warn her;[48] or (3) he may be understood as speaking to himself and therefore the direct discourse may be introduced by a verb meaning "to think," for example "Boaz thought to himself."[49] The first interpretation seems rather unlikely, for nothing has been said previously about the servants' noticing Ruth's presence at the threshing floor. If Boaz wanted to address this statement to the servants, it is strange that the Hebrew text would not have indicated clearly to whom the statement was made. In the case of the second interpretation, it would be necessary to alter the direct discourse so as to read "no one must know that you came here." Accordingly, it is probable that the third interpretation is to be accepted. This interpretation may also suggest that, since Boaz had concluded that no one must know that she was there, he had told her to get up before it was light enough for her to be seen.[50] The entire verse may then be restructured as:

"So she slept at his feet until morning. Since Boaz had concluded that no one should know that she (or this woman, or a woman[51]) had come there, he told her to get up when it was still dark so that no one would recognize her."

3.15   Boaz said to her, "Take off your cloak and spread it out here." She did, and he poured out almost a hundred pounds of barley, and helped her pick it up. Then she returned to town with it.

The Hebrew text has only "he said," but it is usually necessary at this point to be quite specific that it is Boaz who speaks to Ruth. Therefore, the TEV has Boaz said to her.[52]

The Hebrew word translated here as cloak occurs only in this passage and in Isaiah 3.22. Early translations usually employ a rendering such as "mantle" (RSV, Moffatt, Smith-Goodspeed), whereas more recent translations tend to prefer "cloak" (NAB, NEB, TEV). It is clear from the weight that she was to carry in this garment that it could not have been a thin veil. Probably it was a loose, sleeveless outer garment of relatively heavy cloth[53] and therefore appropriate to use in carrying a heavy load of barley.

Almost a hundred pounds of barley translates a Hebrew expression which is simply "six (measures) of barley." There is no specific indication in the Hebrew text as to what measure is involved, but the ellipsis of words for measure is quite frequent in Hebrew.[54] It is possible to say "six measures of barley" (RSV, NAB, NEB), but this is not very useful in determining the amount involved. Some scholars[55] believe that this is a reference to the ephah, but six ephah would amount to approximately 240 liters (well over 500 pounds), an impossible load for Ruth to carry back to the city. It is possible that the measurement was a se'ah (one-third of an ephah) in which case the total capacity would be approximately 80 liters (about 200 pounds). Since some have felt that even this was too heavy a weight for Ruth to carry, this hypothesis has not found large support.[56] Others have concluded that the measure was an 'omer, which would be equal to one-tenth of an ephah, or approximately 24 liters (somewhat over 50 pounds). This is the interpretation accepted by a majority of modern scholars.[57] It does seem important to indicate that this was an impressive amount of barley —not merely from the fact that Boaz had to help her lift it, but because it was evidently designed to impress both Ruth and Naomi with Boaz's generosity and his determination to help them in every way that he could.

The majority of Hebrew manuscripts actually have "he (that is, Boaz) went back to town," but the feminine form also occurs in some Hebrew manuscripts, and the reading "she went back to town" is preferred by a majority of modern scholars and translators.[58]

According to verse 3, Ruth went down to the threshing-floor. Her return to town implies the opposite movement, "Ruth went up to town." For languages in which careful distinctions in geographical movement are specified, it is important to reflect this detail.

3.16a   She went to her mother-in-law, who asked her, "How did you get along, daughter?"

In Hebrew Naomi's question to Ruth is "Who are you, my daughter?" This could be interpreted as Naomi's question as Ruth knocked at her door.[59] Most scholars, however, believe that the interrogative pronoun "who" is to be interpreted as a question about Ruth's condition or circumstances.[60] Hence, in English one could render this Hebrew question as How did you get along?, "How did things go with you?," or "How did things turn out for you?" In some receptor languages it may even be necessary to employ a more specific question such as "How did Boaz receive you?" or "How did you make out with Boaz?"

As in other passages in the Book of Ruth, Naomi's use of the phrase my daughter may need to be changed in some languages to "my daughter-in-law" or "my dear one."

> Ruth told her everything that Boaz had done for her. [17]She added, "He told me I must not come back to you empty-handed, so he gave me all this barley."
> [18]Naomi said to her, "Now be patient, Ruth, until you see how this will turn out. Boaz will not rest today until he settles the matter."

These final paragraphs of chapter 3 (verses 16b-18) summarize the contents and the basic theme of the chapter, namely, the way in which Boaz treated Ruth, not only in the promise which he made to her, but also in the tangible evidence of his generosity and determination to help her by giving her such a large amount of barley. Verse 18 not only serves to tie the whole chapter together by reintroducing Naomi's assurances to Ruth, but it serves as a transition to chapter 4, since it introduces the fact that the legal procedures will take place immediately.

3.16b-17   Ruth told her everything that Boaz had done for her. (17) She added, "He told me I must not come back to you empty-handed, so he gave me all this barley."

It is important to indicate that Ruth communicated more to Naomi than simply the contents of verse 17. Evidently, she described to Naomi everything that Boaz had done for her, and then she added what is recorded in verse 17. For this reason the TEV introduces the direct quotation in verse 17 by She added. One may also use some such expression as "She also said," "In addition she said," or "Furthermore, she said."

All this barley translates the Hebrew expression "these six measures of barley" (see comments on 3.15), and most modern translations follow a literal rendering of the Hebrew text. In this context the emphasis is not upon the exact measure, but upon the unusually large quantity of barley, thus symbolizing Boaz's generosity and his concern for Ruth and Naomi. Some persons have even seen in this gift a kind of dowry. [61] At any rate, Naomi's confidence in the happy ending to the events is certainly reinforced by this rich gift. In order to show the relation between the gift and Naomi's confidence, it is important to emphasize the quantity: <u>all this barley</u>. One may also employ such expressions as "so much barley" or "this large load of barley."

<u>3.18</u>   Naomi said to her, "Now be patient, Ruth, until you see how this will turn out. Boaz will not rest today until he settles the matter."

<u>Be patient</u> translates what is literally in Hebrew "sit down," with emphasis upon being quiet and unworried. The implicit location is "here" and therefore one may translate, as in the NAB: "wait here." However, the focus of attention is not so much upon the location as upon the attitude which Naomi thinks Ruth is justified in having. Accordingly, a translation such as <u>be patient</u> (as in the TEV) is recommended. One may also use a negative equivalent, for example, "do not worry" or "do not be concerned."

<u>How this will turn out</u> is a very general expression and may be rendered as "what will happen," "what will be the result," "what will happen to you," or "what will happen which concerns you."

<u>Will turn out</u> must suggest that the results will be known very shortly, and therefore in languages which have more than one future tense, it is important to use a future which designates activity or an event of the same day.

<u>Will not rest until he settles</u> may be altered into an affirmative expression: "he will certainly settle," "he will surely take care of," or "he will most surely arrange for."

CHAPTER 4

Boaz Marries Ruth

4 Boaz went to the meeting place at the town gate, and sat down there. Then Elimelech's nearest relative, the man whom Boaz had mentioned, came by, and Boaz called to him, "Come over here, my friend, and sit down." So he went over and sat down. ²Then Boaz got ten of the town's leaders and asked them to sit down there too. When they were seated, ³he said to his relative, "Now that Naomi has come back from Moab, she wants to sell the field that belonged to our relative Elimelech, ⁴and I think you ought to know about it. Now then, if you want it, buy it in the presence of these men sitting here. But if you don't want it, say so, because the right to buy it belongs first to you, and then to me."

The man said, "I will buy it."

⁵Boaz said, "Now then, if you buy the field from Naomi, then Ruth,ᵇ the Moabite widow, becomes your wife, so that the field will stay in the dead man's family."

⁶The man answered, "In that case I will give up my right to buy the field, because it might mean that my own children would inherit less. You buy it; I would rather not."

ᵇ *Some ancient translations* then Ruth; *Hebrew* and from Ruth, and she.

There are three principal parts to chapter 4: (1) the legal proceeding (verses 1-12), (2) a conclusion which focuses upon the birth of Obed (verses 13-17), and (3) a genealogy (verses 18-22). Verse 7 is an explanation of the way in which certain aspects of buying and exchanging property were symbolized by taking off a sandal. This provides a useful break in the first section and also introduces the next phase of the legal proceeding, described in verses 9-12.

The opening verses of chapter 4 consist primarily of two parts. The first part (vv. 1-2) constitutes the setting in which Boaz takes his place and then arranges for the participation of Elimelech's nearest relative and of the ten elders of the town. The second part (vv. 3-6) consists of the dialogue between Boaz and Elimelech's nearest relative. The crisis or turning point in this dialogue is at the end of verse 4 and the beginning of verse 5. Boaz first cleverly maneuvers Elimelech's nearest relative into saying that he will buy the field and then presents the man with an impossible condition, thus forcing him to withdraw his offer.

The title Boaz Marries Ruth is probably the most satisfactory title for this entire chapter, though in many languages one cannot use a present tense but must use a past tense: "Boaz Married Ruth." It is possible to divide the chapter by having Boaz Marries Ruth at the beginning, with a subsection beginning at verse 13 entitled "The Birth of a Son," "Ruth Gives Birth to Obed," or "Ruth Has a Son." It is also possible to have a final section heading just preceding the genealogy (vv. 18-22). This could be entitled "The Family Line of David" or possibly "The Ancestors and Descendants of Obed" or "The Ancestors and Descendants of Boaz." However, the focus is upon David, and therefore it would probably be better to mention his name in the title, if one is employed: "The Ancestors of David" or "The Family Line of David."

4.1   Boaz went to the meeting place at the town gate, and sat down
there. Then Elimelech's nearest relative, the man whom Boaz had
mentioned, came by, and Boaz called to him, "Come over here, my
friend, and sit down." So he went over and sat down.

The verb employed in the phrase Boaz went is in the perfect tense, and this
would indicate that the action described in this verse is not necessarily consecutive or following what has been mentioned at the end of chapter 3. Naomi's reply
to Ruth, however, would seem to indicate that this is the next action, since she
assures Ruth that "Boaz will settle the matter today." Nevertheless, the action
described in verse 1 could have taken place earlier, at the same time, or later
than the last events mentioned in chapter 3.[1] In some languages some marker of
sequence of action is almost always required. A rendering such as "meanwhile"
(Smith-Goodspeed) would seem to be too explicit. The NEB has "now Boaz had
gone," which would seem to place the action prior to what was recorded at the
end of chapter 3. In some languages one is almost required to employ some such
expression as "and then," which does not necessarily mark consecutive action
but indicates that this is the next event being related in the story.

In languages which consistently mark certain aspects of direction, the verb
went can be more specifically indicated as "went up," since this is the meaning
of the Hebrew expression; but it would be wrong to try to force this type of meaning too specifically at this point.

To the meeting place at the town gate is in Hebrew merely "to the gate,"
but a literal rendering would have very little meaning for the average reader.
In the first place, people do not think in terms of a gate to a city. Furthermore,
the mention of merely a "gate" would imply some ordinary gate within the city
and not "the city gate." Therefore it is important to specify what kind of gate is
involved (see NEB, Moffatt, Smith-Goodspeed). The addition of the qualification
"city" to "gate" has already been done by early translators.[2] In many languages
it is not enough to state "city gate," since this too would be relatively meaningless. One must specify the relation between the gate and the city, for example,
"the gate leading into the city" or "the gate by which people went in and out of
the city." But what is significant in this context is not the gate itself, but the
space immediately inside the town gate which was so important to the social life
of the city. It was here that judgments were normally held (Deuteronomy 21.19;
25.7; etc.). One must, therefore, in many languages add some such expression
as "the meeting place," so as to indicate clearly the relevant components which
occur in the word "gate" used in this kind of context.

The expansion of the Hebrew term "the gate" to a phrase such as the meeting place at the town gate might seem to be an unwarranted addition, but this
phrase only makes explicit what is fully implicit in the meaningful components
of the Hebrew term "gate." In this context the meaning of "gate" is not the particular structure in the town wall, but the area inside the gate which was used
for important consultations.

In many societies there are no gates to a city; and if there are gates, the
area immediately inside the gate may be of no importance to the life of the com-

munity. In some societies the closest equivalent may be "the chief's compound," where the chief speaks to the people and supervises legal proceedings and where the people of the village often gather for social occasions. In other societies, the functional equivalent is the public square or courtyard, often spoken of as "the plaza," and generally distinct from the market place.[3] For the culture of the Bible the gate was so important that one should avoid, if at all possible, making a complete cultural adaptation by using an expression such as "the chief's compound." It is far better to employ something like "to the public square at the town gate" or "to the gathering place of the city near the city gates."

Elimelech's nearest relative is literally in Hebrew "he who has the right of redemption." For an analysis of this expression, see the comments on 2.20 and 3.12. One may use in the present context a designation of proximity in the family line, for example, "he stands closest to Elimelech in the family" or "he sits closer to Elimelech in the family than Boaz did." Or one may use some designation to indicate function, for example, "he is the first one who should help out as a relative," "he is the one who has the first right to take Ruth as a wife," or "he is the first one who should help Naomi and Ruth."

If the levirate marriage arrangement is the basis for Boaz's marriage to Ruth,[4] there are only two passages in the Old Testament outside of the Book of Ruth which deal specifically with the subject: Genesis 38 and Deuteronomy 25.5-10. (References to both of these passages are included within this chapter; see comments on verses 8 and 12.) The passage in Deuteronomy speaks only about a widow's relation to her brother-in-law, but in the Genesis passage there is an indication that the levirate relation is not limited to the brother-in-law, and when a brother-in-law does not exist, another relative may serve. It may be that the text in Deuteronomy suggests a restriction of something that had a wider practice in earlier times, and that it is this wider practice which is reflected in the Book of Ruth.[5]

The man whom Boaz had mentioned may need to be somewhat more specific in some languages, for example, "it was to Ruth that Boaz had mentioned this man" or "Boaz had mentioned to Ruth this person." If the expression the man whom Boaz had mentioned must be made a separate sentence, it would normally occur after the sentence "just then Elimelech's nearest relative came by."

The Hebrew expression rendered in the TEV as my friend literally means "another, an unknown person."[6] This type of expression is used when an author does not wish to mention or cannot name the specific person or place involved in an account. These words are not specifically included in the statement by Boaz, but come from the author of the book. This means that the name of the person involved was not known to the tradition, or that the author simply did not wish to invent a name. It is possible that the person was well known and that the author intentionally omitted his name in order not to embarrass a well-known person.[7] It is also possible that the author had no interest in preserving the name, as there is no emphasis upon this particular relative.[8] In the two other places in the Old Testament where this expression occurs (1 Samuel 21.2; 2 Kings 6.8) the name is omitted deliberately. Earlier translators already encountered problems with the translation of this term,[9] and in some instances it may be very difficult indeed to find some natural equivalent.[10] In view of the fact that these words do not actually form a part of Boaz's speech, it is possible to omit them (cf. Smith-Goodspeed), but in many instances it seems far more natural and polite to have some kind of expression of address such as "sir." In some cases a rendering such as "my friend" appears to be even more satisfactory.

It is important in introducing the last sentence of verse 1 to employ some kind of particle marking result, for example, "so," "as a result," or even "hence." This marks the sentence as the conclusion or result of what has immediately preceded.

4.2　　　Then Boaz got ten of the town's leaders and asked them to sit down there too. When they were seated,

The Hebrew text of verse 2 begins "and he took ten men of the elders of the city." Since, however, Elimelech's nearest relative is the subject of the last sentence of verse 1, it is normally important to mark the shift of actors so that Boaz should be introduced as the subject of the first sentence of verse 2. The fact that this action by Boaz is subsequent to the preceding should be marked by some kind of transitional device such as then, "and next," or "immediately afterwards."

Certain problems are involved in translating the verb got, which represents in Hebrew a verb often translated as "took." One should not imagine that Boaz had to go through the town in order to find or select ten of the town's elders; what he no doubt did was to ask ten of the town's elders to stop as they were going in or out of the town gate. In many languages an appropriate translation would be "and Boaz caused ten of the town elders to stop" or "Boaz asked ten of the town elders to remain." It is also possible to use an expression such as "selected" or "picked out" (cf. NAB), but this might imply too formal an activity.

The leaders mentioned in this context would have been the heads of leading families, who formed the aristocracy of the town. As local authorities they were largely responsible for legal matters (see Deuteronomy 25.7; 1 Kings 21.8-14).[11] There would certainly have been more than ten elders in Bethlehem, though the exact number is not known. A town such as Sukkoth had seventy-seven elders, according to Judges 8.14. In finding an appropriate term for "elders," it is important not to use a word which merely means "older men," though in many societies the older men are the leaders of the town. A more natural expression in many languages is "ten important men in the town," "ten of the leaders in the town," or "ten of the men in the town to whom people showed respect."

The direct discourse employing an imperative expression, as in the Hebrew, "said, 'Sit down here,'" might seem to be rather impolite in some languages. For that reason, the TEV introduces indirect discourse, asked them to sit down, which may seem more natural in such a setting. If direct discourse is used, the imperative force of the request may be somewhat altered by the use of some particle showing proper politeness, equivalent to "please" in English: "please sit down here."

When they were seated translates what is literally in Hebrew: "and they sat down." If an independent clause is used, it should be observed that their sitting down is a result of Boaz's request, and therefore it must be rendered as "so they sat down" or "hence they sat down."

4.3   he said to his relative, "Now that Naomi has come back from Moab, she wants to sell the field that belonged to our relative Elimelech,

The identification of his relative must be the same as the phrase used in verse 1. It is very awkward in many languages to keep referring to a person without some proper name, but there is no alternative in the present discourse.

The statement of Boaz is literally in Hebrew: "Naomi, who has come back from the country of Moab, is selling the parcel of land which belonged to our kinsman Elimelech." The TEV restructures these principal clauses into a cause-effect or reason-result relation, indicating that in view of the fact that Naomi has come back from Moab, she wanted to sell the field. One of the difficulties in translating this sentence is that this information is entirely new. There is no suggestion, for example, that Boaz had talked to Naomi about this subject. It may be that Boaz simply introduced the question of the land in order to pose this as the first problem or aspect of the negotiation. Such a procedure would certainly be a clever one.[12]

In some languages it is important to indicate that the nearest relative would no doubt know about the field, and therefore the verse may be restructured as "then he said to the nearest relative: You will remember the field that belonged to our relative Elimelech. Naomi has now returned from the country of Moab and she wants to sell it" (cf. NEB).

The field that belonged to our relative Elimelech may be translated as "the field which our deceased relative Elimelech formerly owned."

Our relative Elimelech may be rendered as "Elimelech who was a member of our family," "Elimelech who belonged to our clan," "Elimelech who was related to us," or "Elimelech who was one of our kin."

The Hebrew verb translated wants to sell is normally read as a participle "is selling."[13] The form of the perfect tense (which is the form occurring in the Hebrew text) would normally be translated as "she had sold the field." This would seem to imply that the land had already been sold and that it would need to be bought back from the actual owner. But in verse 9 Boaz buys the land directly from Naomi. It is not necessary, however, to understand the perfect tense in Hebrew as expressing some past event; it can indicate the fact that a decision to sell and the actual act of selling take place at the same time.[14] An appropriate translation in such a case would be "she wants to sell."

4.4   and I think you ought to know about it. Now then, if you want it, buy it in the presence of these men sitting here. But if you don't want it, say so, because the right to buy it belongs first to you, and then to me."
     The man said, "I will buy it."

The clause and I think you ought to know about it is in Hebrew literally "and

I thought I would uncover your ear." The Hebrew verb often translated "thought" is in this context much better translated as "I have decided." To "uncover the ear" is merely a figure of speech meaning "to inform."[15] It would be interesting to retain this metaphor or to use a similar metaphor in a receptor language, but rarely can one do so.[16] Sometimes an approximate expression may be employed, for example, "to open your ears" or "to cause your ears to hear."

Now then...then to me, is a rather complex construction in Hebrew. It could be translated somewhat literally as "saying, buy (it) in the presence of those sitting (here) and in the presence of the elders of my people. If you will redeem (it), redeem (it); but if you will not redeem (it),[17] tell me, that I may know, for there is no one beside you to redeem (it), and I am after you."

This structure can be followed somewhat literally by interpreting the first verb of "saying" as "suggesting," that is "suggesting that you buy it" (see Smith-Goodspeed). This type of rendering depends, however, to some extent upon the rendering of the verb "redeem." If the verb which in Hebrew is often translated "redeem" is translated as "to help out as a relative" or "to do your duty as a relative," one can translate "if you want to do your duty as a relative, then do so" (cf. NEB). In this particular context the specific duty of the relative was to buy the land, and therefore in many languages it is more satisfactory to follow the TEV and translate buy it in the presence of these men sitting here. It is also possible to combine the concept of being a relative with the buying of the land, by translating "if you want to do your duty as a relative in buying the land," but this may turn out to be a rather heavy construction in some languages.

There may be confusion about the references of the word it in verse 4. In the first instance (to know about it), it may refer either to the field or to the fact that Naomi wanted to sell the field. In some languages one must make the reference specific, either as "I have decided to tell you about the field" or "...that Naomi wants to sell the field." The second it (if you want it) is best rendered as "the field," for example, "if you want the field." The third and following uses of it are all references to the field. In some languages "the field" must be used in all instances, but in most cases some kind of pronominal reference to the field is more natural.

Say so is better translated in some languages as "tell me" or even "tell us," since the elders who were present served as witnesses to this agreement or transaction.

The right to buy it belongs first to you may need to be somewhat restructured as "you are the first one to have the right to buy it" or "you come ahead of me in being able to buy it."

The man said is more appropriately translated in some languages as "the man responded," since his statement is in response to the offer of Boaz.

I will buy it involves a form of the Hebrew verb which indicates a rather weak answer, not a particularly firm or definite one.[18] This subtly suggests that he may want to back out of the arrangement, even as he does in verse 6.

4.5   Boaz said, "Now then, if you buy the field from Naomi, then Ruth,
the Moabite widow, becomes your wife, so that the field will stay in
the dead man's family."

A particle such as now then to introduce the direct discourse in verse 5 is
particularly important, not only to mark the sequence of events, but to show at
this particular point an abrupt shift in the argumentation. In some languages it
might be appropriate to have a particle before Boaz said which would suggest
something like "then to everyone's surprise" or "but then." This may be very
useful in marking the complete change in Boaz's presentation of the issue.

Then Ruth, the Moabite widow, becomes your wife is in Hebrew literally
"you are also acquiring (from) Ruth the Moabitess,[19] the dead man's (wife)."
Some English translations prefer to retain the verb "buying," so that they render
"you are also buying Ruth" (RSV, Moffatt, Smith-Goodspeed). It is the same
Hebrew verb used in the expression buy the field, but this Hebrew verb does not
mean specifically "buy" in both contexts, for in Hebrew societies one did not
"buy" a wife. The appropriate meaning of this verb in the second context is "to
acquire."

Essentially the nearest relative had two distinct responsibilities: one was
to preserve the estate of Elimelech (this would be done by buying the field in
order to keep it in the family), and the other was to acquire the widow of Elimelech's son Mahlon.[20]

For the Hebrew phrase "the dead man's (wife)" the focus is upon the wife,
and therefore "widow" is an appropriate translation leaving "the dead man's" as
implicit information.

When the Hebrew text says "you are also acquiring Ruth," this is equivalent
to saying "you must marry Ruth." This aspect of the obligation is expressed in
the TEV simply as then Ruth, the Moabite widow, becomes your wife.

So that the field will stay in the dead man's family is in Hebrew literally
"in order to raise the name of the dead to his inheritance." Basically there are
two ideas combined in this Hebrew expression. (1) The aim of the levirate marriage was "to raise children for the dead." In this way a man was given a kind
of continuing life through his sons. (2) The name of the dead is restored to his
inheritance through the fact that the property becomes the property of the child
of the widow who is married, rather than becoming the personal asset of the one
who acquires the property on behalf of the dead husband. In other words, the
property would belong not to the closest relative, but to the son of the widow.
Furthermore, the son would be regarded as the son of the widow's deceased husband rather than as the son of the person who had redeemed the property and
married the widow. By fulfilling the responsibility of the closest kin, a person
would in essence be diminishing his own property right and estate, and thus de-
priving his other children of a portion of their inheritance.

In order to make all of these aspects quite explicit, one could translate
this passage as "you must also marry Ruth, the Moabite widow, and you must
raise children by her so that the field will stay in the dead man's family."

4.6   The man answered, "In that case I will give up my right to buy the field, because it might mean that my own children would inherit less. You buy it; I would rather not."

The man answered may be rendered as "the near relative replied" (NAB) or simply "he answered." As in most instances there would be no doubt as to who is speaking.

I will give up my right to buy the field is literally in Hebrew "I cannot redeem for myself." This could also be rendered as "I cannot help out as a relative" or "I cannot do my duty as a relative." It may even be possible to employ a more specific rendering such as "I cannot take Ruth as a wife" or "I cannot buy the field." This will depend largely upon the expressions which have been used for "redemption" in earlier contexts.

Because it might mean that my own children would inherit less is somewhat more explicit than the Hebrew text itself "in order that I may not ruin my own inheritance." Compare also the NEB "for I should risk losing my own patrimony" and Moffatt "for fear of injuring my own inheritance." It is also possible to translate simply as "because I would impoverish myself," "because I would make myself poor," or "because I myself would then become poor."

Lose my own inheritance could be translated merely as "lose what I have inherited" or "lose what I now possess."

Will be in danger of may be rendered in some languages as "will run the risk of," "would likely," or "would no doubt."

You buy it reflects a Hebrew phrase: "take my right of redemption yourself, for I cannot redeem." This phrase presents a number of difficulties in some languages and thus requires considerable restructuring, for example, "you buy the field just as I would have bought it but cannot," "you can now buy the field though I cannot," or "you yourself do what I cannot do, that is, you buy the field."

I would rather not may be rendered as "I do not wish to buy the field" or "I prefer not to buy the field."

⁷Now this is what they used to do in Israel to settle a sale or exchange of property: the seller would take off his sandal and give it to the buyer. This was the way Israelites showed that the matter was settled.

⁸So when the man said to Boaz, "You buy it," he took off his sandal and gave it to him.^c ⁹Then Boaz said to the leaders and all the others there, "You are all witnesses today that I have bought from Naomi everything that belonged to Elimelech, and to Chilion and Mahlon. ¹⁰In addition, Ruth the Moabite, Mahlon's widow, becomes my wife. This will keep the property in the dead man's family, and his family line will continue among his people and in his hometown. You are witnesses to this today."

¹¹The leaders and the others said, "Yes, we are witnesses. May the Lord make this woman, who is coming into your home, to be like Rachel and Leah, who bore many children to Jacob. May you become rich in the clan of Ephrath, and famous in Bethlehem. ¹²May the children that the Lord will give you by this young woman make your family to be like the family of Perez, the son of Judah and Tamar."

^c *One ancient translation* and gave it to him; *Hebrew omits.*

[69]

4.7

     Verse 7 contains a brief explanation of an earlier custom in Israel. This break in the narrative seems necessary to the writer in order that the reader may understand what will be related in verses 8 and 9. Verses 9 and 10 contain primarily the statement of Boaz to the elders and all others who were present, while verses 11 and 12 are the response of the people, not only as witnesses to the event, but as those who wish to express their blessing on the marriage of Ruth to Boaz.

<u>4.7</u>   Now this is what they used to do in Israel to settle a sale or exchange of property: the seller would take off his sandal and give it to the buyer. This was the way Israelites showed that the matter was settled.

     The text of this verse in Hebrew is literally "and this was (the custom)[21] in former times in Israel concerning redeeming and exchanging: to confirm[22] a transaction, the one drew off his sandal and gave it to the other, and this was (the manner of) attesting in Israel." In rendering this verse it is necessary in a number of languages to make certain aspects explicit. One must often indicate clearly what are the objects of redeeming and exchanging. The TEV does this by stating <u>a sale or exchange of property</u>, and then makes both parties explicit by speaking of <u>seller</u> and <u>buyer</u>. This interprets the ceremony of the shoe as a general witness of a contract for the sale of property. This is a possible interpretation and it is defended by some commentators.[23] It may be, however, that the ceremony involving the shoe is not a general one to mark the sale of property, but it may be restricted to situations involving relatives and the abandonment of one's normal responsibility or the transfer of the right of a relative to acquire property on behalf of a dead person. If that is the case, the near relative neither bought nor sold anything; it was only later that Boaz bought the property from Naomi, and in that instance there is no indication of the ceremony of passing a shoe. It is possible that the shoe was regarded as a kind of symbol of power in Israel, as elsewhere,[24] and the taking off the sandal or shoe indicated the surrendering of power or rights. Within the Old Testament, the throwing of a sandal upon a piece of land did mean taking possession of it (Psalm 60.8*), and in the present instance the reversal of the process is true: taking off the sandal meant abandonment of any right to the property.[25] It is, therefore, somewhat dangerous to be too explicit in rendering this verse, and it may be preferable to translate: "whenever property was acquired and rights exchanged" or "whenever people took property or exchanged rights to property." For the same reason, it may be preferable to state "a man" and "the other (party)" instead of <u>seller</u> and <u>buyer</u>.

     <u>This was the way Israelites showed that the matter was settled</u> may require certain modifications in some languages, for example, "the people of Israel had this custom of showing that a matter was settled," "...a transaction was finished," "...the agreement was final," or "...that the people had decided."

---

*Psalm 60.10 in the Hebrew text.

The inclusion of the information in verse 7 indicates that this practice was not widely known at the time the Book of Ruth was written; otherwise it would not have been necessary to introduce this explanation. The necessity for making this kind of explanation concerning an apparently widespread custom of earlier times would suggest a considerable lapse of time between the events described and their being put into the literary form of this book.

4.8   So when the man said to Boaz, "You buy it," he took off his sandal and gave it to him.

The introductory particle translated so may be rendered in some languages as "accordingly." The action in verse 8 illustrates exactly the custom described in 7. The relation between the two verses may be indicated by "in accordance with this" or "just like that."

The imperative expression You buy it may be more appropriately expressed as permission in some languages, for example, "You may buy it yourself," "It is now your privilege to buy it," "It is now your responsibility to buy it," or "It is now up to you to buy it."

There may be certain problems involved in obtaining a satisfactory rendering for sandal. Sometimes a term for sandal indicates the footwear of particularly poor persons or, in some situations, footwear used only for recreation or sport. If this is the case, it would be better to use a general designation for footwear which would include sandals.

The final phrase of verse 8, and gave it to him, does not occur in the Hebrew text, but it is attested by some early translations.[26] This phrase may reflect the wording of a similar expression in verse 7,[27] but it may also indicate that an original Hebrew phrase has been lost.[28] Regardless of what may or may not have been the original Hebrew text, in some languages the narrative style requires such an addition. One may also wish to add at this point a marginal note to indicate that this phrase occurs in some ancient Greek manuscripts but is lacking in the Hebrew text.[29]

4.9   Then Boaz said to the leaders and all the others there, "You are all witnesses today that I have bought from Naomi everything that belonged to Elimelech, and to Chilion and Mahlon.

The sequence of events is clearly marked here by the particle then, which may be rendered somewhat more specifically in some languages as "and next" or "and after that."

And all the others there is in Hebrew literally "and all the people."[30] This does not refer to all the people of the town, but to "all the people present" or "all those who were there." This is appropriately rendered in English as all the others there.

You are all witnesses today may be translated literally in some languages as "you have all seen today." In other languages, however, the role of a witness must be explained not only in terms of what people have seen, but also what they can later confirm, for example, "You have all seen today that I have bought from

Naomi everything that belonged to Elimelech and to Chilion and Mahlon, and later you can tell folks that you have seen this happen" or "you have all seen today, and later you can explain how I have bought from Naomi everything...."

That I have bought indicates that the action belongs to the past, but the Hebrew tense of the verb shows quite clearly that this is an action which is accomplished at the very moment the words are spoken[31] (cf. Smith-Goodspeed "I am buying").

From Naomi is in Hebrew literally "at (from) the hand of Naomi." This is a typical Hebrew idiom which can rarely be translated literally into other languages. The "hand" is a symbol for possession.

The relation of Chilion and Mahlon to the property is somewhat different from that of Elimelech, since the two sons inherited from their father. This must be made somewhat more explicit in some languages as "everything that belonged first to Elimelech, and accordingly to Chilion and Mahlon" or, even more explicitly, "everything that belonged first to Elimelech and then to his sons, Chilion and Mahlon."

4.10 In addition, Ruth the Moabite, Mahlon's widow, becomes my wife. This will keep the property in the dead man's family, and his family line will continue among his people and in his hometown. You are witnesses to this today."

The phrase in addition may be rendered in some languages as "also," but a fuller form may be required in certain instances, for example, "in addition to the property" or "but after the property also."

It may be useful in this context to retain the expression the Moabite, perhaps in the form "the woman from Moab" or "the Moabite woman," so as to emphasize satisfactorily the fact that Ruth was not of Jewish background.

For the translation of becomes my wife, see the comment on verse 5.

For the expression this will keep the property in the dead man's family, see the notes on verse 5. It would be wrong, however, to suggest that Ruth becomes the wife of Boaz only in order to keep the property in the dead man's family. Hence, it may be useful to indicate clearly that this is a type of result, for example, "and as a result the property will remain in the dead man's family" or "...in the family of Mahlon."

And his family line will continue among his people is literally in Hebrew "that the name of the dead may not be cut off from among his brethren." The TEV changes the passive expression to an active one and eliminates the rather difficult figurative expression "cut off from among" (a very common Hebrew figure).

In some languages it is essential to specify whose name is involved. This could be "the name of Mahlon." But the focus throughout this passage has been upon the relationship of the various persons to Elimelech, and therefore one may translate: "the name of Elimelech."

In a number of languages one cannot speak about a "name continuing," but it may be possible to employ some related expression, such as "that the name of Elimelech will not be missing (lacking, failing) among his brothers."

For some languages the whole concept of name as a substitute for a person (or as in this context, for descendants) may be impossible, and therefore one may translate: "that his descendants will not be lacking" or "that he may have descendants."[32]

In his hometown is literally in Hebrew "from the gate of his place." For the significance of this expression see the comments on 3.11.

You are witnesses to this today may be rendered as "You have seen this today and you can speak of it tomorrow." In this way participating in an event and being able to confirm it at a later time are clearly indicated as the double role of a witness.

4.11-12   The leaders and the others said, "Yes, we are witnesses. May the Lord make this woman, who is coming into your home, to be like Rachel and Leah, who bore many children to Jacob. May you become rich in the clan of Ephrath, and famous in Bethlehem. (12) May the children that the Lord will give you by this young woman make your family to be like the family of Perez, the son of Judah and Tamar."

The statement of all the people present is essentially a kind of blessing, and it typically has a poetic structure. Verse 11 consists of three lines with a meter $3 + 2$, $2 + 3$, $3 + 3$. A literal translation corresponding to the line divisions would be: // The Lord make this woman / who is coming into your house // like Rachel and Leah / who built up the house of Israel. // Prosper in Ephrathah / be renowned in Bethlehem. //

Verse 12 also has a poetic structure consisting of two lines with the meter $2 + 2 + 3$, $3 + 2 + 2$. A literal rendering by line and phrase would be: // May your house be / like the house of Perez / whom Tamar bore to Judah, // thanks to the children that will give / you the Lord / by this young woman. // It would be excellent if a translation could reflect this type of poetic structure, but that is usually quite difficult. The passage is too short to establish a well-recognized structure, and the content does not lend itself to poetic formulation, since it does not have the normal wealth of figurative expression. Furthermore, it is in the form of a prayer or request and is thus more difficult to render into poetic form.

As in so many instances, an expression beginning with may the Lord make this woman must be introduced in a manner that will show that this is direct discourse addressed to the Lord, for example, "We pray that the Lord will make this woman."

Though some make a distinction between the response of the people in being witnesses and the blessing of the elders and thus follow early translation evidence which has sometimes been defended as the right reading,[33] the Hebrew text itself reads "all the people who were at the gate and the elders said," followed by the statement concerning witnessing the event as well as the blessing. Such a division is regarded by others as being artificial.[34] But a literal rendering of the Hebrew text is likewise awkward, since a clause "who were at the gate" is hardly necessary in this context. The fact that other people in addition to the elders were sitting in the meeting place at the town gate was already introduced in verse 4.

Since the question concerning the witnessing of this event has already been posed indirectly in verse 10, it may be more satisfactory to begin verse 11 by the leaders and the others said, Yes. If verse 10 ends with a question, "Do you witness this today?" one can have the answer, "We do so" (NAB).

Who bore many children to Jacob is in Hebrew literally "who built up the house of Israel." The expression "build a house" is a metaphor to describe perpetuating or establishing a family line,[35] but in most languages it is quite impossible to equate a house with a lineage, and therefore some type of adaptation such as the TEV employs is necessary. Or it may be necessary to say: "who gave birth to many children, who in turn became the people of Israel." In other languages it may be possible to say: "who were the ancestresses of the Israelites," "who were the ancient mothers of the Israelites," or "who were the mothers of olden times for the Israelites."

The transcription of the proper names Rachel and Leah should follow the general principles mentioned in the comments on 1.1. The mention of Rachel is particularly appropriate in this context, since the tradition concerning Rachel was associated with Bethlehem (Genesis 35.19-20).

The term rich in the expression may you become rich in the clan of Ephrath involves three essential components of meaning: might, moral value, and wealth. Some translators and commentators emphasize the first component;[36] others, the second;[37] but the majority of translators employ terms which focus upon the third component, namely, wealth.[38] In general, it is best to follow this interpretation of the term, since it is this aspect of the meaning which appears to be in focus in the context. Some scholars would argue that the particular aspect of wealth valid for this context is "children,"[39] but this is an aspect of meaning which, while it may be derived from the text, probably should not be made explicit in a translation.

Famous in Bethlehem is an expression which is parallel to rich in the clan of Ephrath. In Hebrew it is literally "proclaim (your own) name in Bethlehem." This is equivalent to "become famous."[40] Some receptor languages have idioms which are relatively close to the Hebrew, for example, "may you have a good name in Bethlehem," "may all people in Bethlehem know your name," or "may your name be spoken by all in Bethlehem." This type of blessing is still current in the Middle East.[41]

The wish expressed in verse 12 may likewise require some type of introductory statement, such as "we pray that," "we wish that," or "we ask that."

The TEV rendering of verse 12 reverses the sentence order of the Hebrew text by starting out with the basis for the comparison, which in the Hebrew text comes at the end (so also in Smith-Goodspeed, NAB, Bible de Jérusalem, and Dhorme). The TEV order is more natural in many languages, but it may be somewhat complex because of the inclusion of dependent clauses. Therefore one may wish to employ a somewhat different order and statement of relations, for example, "May the Lord give you children by this woman; then your family will be like the family of Perez. He was the son of Judah and Tamar."

It is very difficult in some languages to speak of the Lord giving something by means of someone else. This makes the Lord the primary agent and this young woman becomes the secondary agent. For many languages the only way to express this relation is to say: "that the Lord will cause this young woman to give to you" or "that this young woman will give to you; the Lord will cause it."

An additional complication in verse 12 is that there is a causative expression in the relation of the children to the family, expressed in some languages as "may the children...make your family to be like the family of Perez." In some languages the "likeness" must be expressed in terms of some particular quality, that is to say, it must be like the family of Perez in being large or in being distinguished. Both could be the case, but in view of the special emphasis upon the lineage of David, it would seem that the focus is upon the importance of the family, for example, "may the children...make your family to be important like the family of Perez."

The mention of Perez, son of Judah and Tamar, involves a reference to the levirate union between Judah and Tamar. In that case no marriage was involved, for Tamar's connection with Judah was only legitimate for the purpose of raising children. If the union had been perpetuated, it would have been illegitimate. Perez was the ancestor of the clan of Ephrath, to which Boaz himself belonged. It may, therefore, be important to introduce a footnote at this point to indicate his relation to the family of Perez. This is brought out in the genealogy (vv. 18-22), but it may not be evident to the reader.

The blessing of verse 12 speaks consistently about the family of Boaz and to this extent does not mention the fact that a child born from the marriage of Boaz to Ruth would be technically considered to be the child of Ruth's deceased husband, Mahlon.[42] However, since Boaz and the deceased husband belonged to the same clan, the failure to mention Mahlon is not too important. Furthermore, the whole emphasis of this story is upon the character of Boaz and his faithfulness to the traditions of Israel.

> [13]So Boaz took Ruth home as his wife. The Lord blessed her, and she became pregnant and had a son. [14]The women said to Naomi, "Praise the Lord! He has given you a grandson today to take care of you. May the boy become famous in Israel! [15]Your daughter-in-law loves you, and has done more for you than seven sons. And now she has given you a grandson, who will bring new life to you and give you security in your old age." [16]Naomi took the child, held him close, and took care of him.
> [17]The women of the neighborhood named the boy Obed. They told everyone, "A son has been born to Naomi!" He became the father of Jesse, who was David's father.

These final paragraphs constitute a conclusion, not only to chapter 4, but to the entire Book of Ruth. In keeping with the theme of emptiness and filling, Naomi now has been completely restored, not only in property rights (while also receiving compensation for the property), but also in the possession of a grandson, who is spoken of as being equivalent to seven sons (v. 15). Part of the treatment of the theme of fullness is to be found in the emphasis upon the fertility of Ruth, in contrast with barrenness.

Verses 14 and 15 are in a sense the high point of this section, and they contrast very well with Naomi's earlier expression of lack (1.20-21).

The focus on Naomi continues through verse 17. Verses 16 and 17 deal with the adoption of the child and the joyous exclamation of the women of the neighborhood, who give a name to the boy.

4.13   So Boaz took Ruth home as his wife. The Lord blessed her, and she became pregnant and had a son.

The introductory particle translated so is particularly important here. It is rendered in some languages as "accordingly," "in accordance with this," or "even as Boaz said he would do."

So Boaz took Ruth home as his wife is an important transitional expression. In a sense it forms a conclusion to what has immediately preceded, since there Boaz declared that he would take Ruth as his wife. It also introduces the contents of verses 13-17, which include Ruth's conception, the birth of the child, and the response of the women to Naomi.

In Hebrew the form of the first clause is literally "so Boaz took Ruth and she became his wife." A literal translation of the Hebrew becomes very complex in some languages, particularly since a verb "took" might very well imply sexual relations. It is far more satisfactory to understand this verb in the sense of "take home" or "lead someone to one's house." It is possible to take this verb in the sense of "to marry" (Bible de Jérusalem), but if that is done, the last part of the clause, "and she became his wife," is completely redundant. It is possible also to coalesce the two expressions into one, as "Boaz married Ruth," and some early translators did understand the verb "take" with this meaning.[43] However, it does seem preferable to understand the first verb as "take home" and the second expression as indicating Ruth's specific relation to Boaz as wife. There is a further value in this translation from the standpoint of the discourse structure in that there is thus a shift in the location of the action.

The TEV leaves implicit a clause which is literally in Hebrew "he went in to her." This is a euphemism for the sexual act and is a frequently employed Hebrew expression (e.g. Genesis 16.2; 30.3; 38.8; Deuteronomy 22.13; 2 Samuel 16.21). Other languages often have parallel euphemistic expressions, for example, "he came near to her,"[44] "he slept with her," "he was joined to her," or "he lay beside her."

It is important to indicate clearly the causative relation in the Lord blessed her, and she became pregnant, since fertility as well as barrenness are often in the Scriptures attributed directly to God (see Genesis 29.31; 30.2; etc.). Sometimes conception is spoken of in a more concrete manner, for example, "the Lord caused her to have a baby in her womb," "the Lord enabled her to receive seed in her womb," or "the Lord caused her to have a child." This last translation would combine conception and birth, the latter being spoken of in the last clause of verse 13.

4.14-15   The women said to Naomi, "Praise the Lord! He has given you a grandson today to take care of you. May the boy become famous in Israel! (15) Your daughter-in-law loves you, and has done more for you than seven sons. And now she has given you a grandson, who will bring new life to you and give you security in your old age."

The women referred to at the beginning of verse 14 are essentially the same women as are spoken of in 1.19. They are the women of the town of Bethlehem, and it may be necessary to specify the fact, for example, "the women of the town" or "the women in Bethlehem."

A literal translation of Praise the Lord! may be quite difficult in some languages. It might appear, for example, to be simply a command to Naomi that she should praise the Lord. In reality it is a general statement that the Lord deserves to be praised because of the events related in the context. The closest equivalent in some languages is "we must all praise the Lord," "we should praise the Lord," or "the Lord is worthy that we should praise him." Terms for praise are quite varied in different languages: "to lift up the name of the Lord," "to make the name of the Lord great," or "to say, The Lord is great."

The blessing contained in verses 14 and 15 has a poetic structure. Verse 14 consists of three lines with the meter 2, 3 + 3, 3, which may be rendered literally as // Blessed be the Lord // who has not left you / without next of kin this day. // May his name be renowned in Israel. // Verse 15 consists of two lines of poetry with the following meter: 3 + 3, 3 + 2 + 2, and may be rendered literally as // May he be to you a restorer of life / and a nourisher of your old age. // Your daughter-in-law who loves you has borne him, / who is more to you / than seven sons. // It would be excellent if this passage could be reproduced in a parallel poetic form in a receptor language. However, as has been noted in other instances of embedded poetry, it is only rarely that such small sections can be satisfactorily reproduced as poetry, both because of their limitation in length and because of their content.

The sentence he has given you a grandson today to take care of you is literally in Hebrew: "who has not left you this day without next of kin." "Next of kin" (or "redeemer") is precisely the same expression which was used of Boaz and the "closer relative" (3.12). Now this expression is applied to the grandson. In most languages it is impossible to speak of a grandson as "next of kin," because such a concept would not fit within most kinship systems. Furthermore, it is not enough to employ an expression such as "heir" (NAB), for this does not do justice to the meaning of the Hebrew term, as one who was obliged to carry out certain responsibilities on behalf of others. The TEV, accordingly, attempts to indicate not only the specific kinship relation, but also the role of such a kin, and thus makes specific the two aspects in the phrase a grandson to take care of you.

It may not be possible to say in some languages he has given you a grandson today. A causative relation may be more appropriate: "he has caused you this day to have a grandson" or "he has caused to be born for you this day a grandson."

May the boy become famous in Israel is in Hebrew literally "that his name be announced." For this type of expression see the comments on verses 11 and 12. Some receptor languages may have an idiom relatively close to the Hebrew: "may he have a good name" or "may his reputation be good." This must, of course, be a reference to the boy and not to the Lord. Nor may it be a reference to the dead man or even to the name of Naomi.[45] In many languages the pronoun "he" would refer directly to the boy, but it may be necessary, as in the TEV, to make this reference explicit.

In some languages become famous in Israel may be expressed as "may the people of Israel all praise him" or "may the people of Israel regard him as great."

In verse 15 the sentence order of the Hebrew text is reversed in the TEV. Such a reversal may be necessary in languages in which events should be described in chronological order.

The term for loves must be carefully selected so that it will be appropriate to the relation between a daughter-in-law and a mother-in-law. In other words, it must be the term to show fond affection between members of a family. It must avoid any implication of sexual interest or concern.

Has done more for you than seven sons is literally in Hebrew "she is better to you than seven sons." Generally this statement requires certain greater explicitness in translation, for example, "she is worth more to you than seven sons" (NAB, Dhorme, Bible de Jérusalem). The TEV refers this statement to the past: has done more for you. Compare also NEB: "who has proved better to you than seven sons." One may compare, for example, Elkanah's question to the childless Hannah: "Am I not more to you than ten sons?" (1 Samuel 1.8). The number seven should not be taken as a sacred number in this context, but simply as a conventional one (cf. 1 Samuel 2.5, "the barren woman has borne seven children"). For that reason, it may be better in some languages to translate: "has done more for you than many sons."

Who will bring new life to you is particularly difficult to translate in some languages. It is usually not satisfactory to employ an expression such as "he will be to you a restorer of life." This might imply that Naomi was dead and that the child would cause her to live again. In some instances the figurative expression of "giving new life to" may need to be somewhat qualified, for example, "may he give you new life, so to speak" or "may he cause you to live a new life, as it were." A more natural expression in many languages is to speak of "restoring strength," for example, "he will give you new strength in your old age" or "he will cause you to be strong even though you are old."

Give you security in your old age may also be rendered as "will support you in your old age,"[46] "will take care of you in your old age," "will see that you have enough when you are old," or "will take care of you when you are old." All of these are expressions of hope which depend for their fulfillment directly or indirectly upon God's blessing. Only in the first sentence of verse 15 is there a direct statement.

4.16   Naomi took the child, held him close, and took care of him.

Naomi took the child may be rendered in some languages as "Naomi took the child in her arms" or "Naomi took the child in her hands."

Held him close is literally in Hebrew "laid him in her bosom" (cf. NEB "laid him in her lap" and NAB "placed him on her lap"). One meaning of the Hebrew term translated "bosom" or "lap" may refer to a fold of the garment at the height of the breast, but this is hardly an appropriate meaning in this context.[47] Most receptor languages have an appropriate way of speaking about this action of taking a child and holding it on the lap or holding it close to oneself. The rendering of the TEV is in this particular context rather neutral.

It is probable that the expression held him close refers to the rite of adoption. Such a rite was well known in the Orient and has been attested in Mesopotamian and Hurrian law in the second millenium B.C. It is not specifically mentioned in the Old Testament laws, but several Old Testament stories suggest that this practice was not unknown in Israel, for example, the adoption of the children of Bilhah and Zilpah by Rachel and Leah in Genesis 30.3-13. There also seem to be traces of such a right in the blessing of Ephraim and Manasseh (Genesis 48) and the fact that the sons of Machir were born on the knees of Joseph (Genesis 50.23). Through a kind of legal adoption symbolized by this act, they were considered the sons of Joseph.[48] This adoption of Obed by Naomi does not necessarily support the argument in favor of an ancient matriarchy which may have preceded a patriarchal organization,[49] nor is the adoption referred to in this passage a typical or ordinary one, since it takes place within the family group and the legal effects would be restricted to the family relationship.[50]

It is not entirely clear whether the Hebrew term underlying the translation and took care of him should be taken literally as "to nurse,"[51] or whether it means simply to look after the child.[52] It would certainly seem better to employ a more general expression such as "and she looked after him," "and she took care of him," or "and she watched after him."

4.17   The women of the neighborhood named the boy Obed. They told everyone, "A son has been born to Naomi!" He became the father of Jesse, who was David's father.

The Hebrew text of verse 17 is literally "and the women of the neighborhood gave him a name, saying, A son has been born to Naomi. They named him Obed; he was the father of Jesse, the father of David." This Hebrew text is rather redundant in its literal form, and therefore some restructuring is necessary in most receptor languages if one is to make the rendering clear and natural. Rather than repeat "gave him a name" and "they named him Obed," it is usually better to translate "the women of the neighborhood named the boy Obed," "they called the boy by the name of Obed," "they said, Obed is his name," or "they declared, Obed will be his name." It is also possible to retain somewhat more of the Hebrew order by translating: "the women of the neighborhood said, A son has been born to Naomi; and they named him Obed." This particular restructuring already exists in an early translation.[53]

It is quite impossible in some languages to say "a son has been born to

Naomi." This would imply that Naomi herself was the mother. The relationship must be changed to read: "Naomi now has a grandson," "a grandson has been born for Naomi," or "Ruth has given birth to a grandson for Naomi."

The name Obed in Hebrew sounds like the word meaning "servant."[54]

In some languages it is impossible to introduce the final sentence of verse 17 without some alteration. A literal translation, "he was the father of Jesse, who was David's father," would be completely confusing since Obed only later became the father of Jesse, who still later became the father of David. Therefore, one must translate this final sentence as "Obed later became the father of Jesse, and Jesse in turn became the father of David." One may also translate as "Obed later had a son who was named Jesse, and Jesse had a son who was named David."

The Family Line of David

[18-22]This is the family line from Perez to David: Perez, Hezron, Ram, Amminadab, Nahshon, Salmon, Boaz, Obed, Jesse, David.

Scholars have seen a number of problems involved in this concluding section to the Book of Ruth, but for the most part those problems are not relevant for the translator.[55] There is, of course, a slight possibility that the genealogy was a kind of afterthought, but genealogies were entirely too important to the Hebrew people to be regarded as something extra or nonessential. In fact, this genealogy may very well be a clue to the significance of the story itself, namely, the fact that David possessed in his own lineage a person of Moabite background. It is possible that this reference is an attempt to correct an ancient tradition concerning the origin of David, which claimed that he had come from the country of Moab. The story of Ruth would show that the family of David was in reality from Bethlehem, and only David's great-grandmother came from Moab. Nevertheless, she had become a Jewess.[56] It is, however, quite impossible on this limited evidence and type of context to determine with any degree of certainty the purpose of the genealogy, except to indicate that it would appear to be an important element, and from the standpoint of Hebrew history and tradition, a fitting conclusion.

The separate title for this final section is useful in that it separates the final verses from the preceding paragraph and to an extent emphasizes the significance of the genealogy.

Since the emphasis in the genealogy is certainly upon David, it is quite appropriate to have as a title The Family Line of David, though, as suggested in the introductory section to this chapter, it would be possible to speak of "The Ancestors and Descendants of Obed."

The proper names should be transliterated on the basis of the general principles already discussed in the comments on 1.1.

The Hebrew text typically employs a verb between each set of names, rendered in traditional translations as "begot." Most later translations into English employ expressions such as "Perez was the father of Hezron, Hezron was the father of Ram," etc. However, this type of genealogy is awkward to read, and it is therefore probably better to employ some such adaptation as in the TEV, which introduces the family line as being from Perez to David and then enumerates the principal person in each generation.

It may be important in this context to have some supplementary note to indicate that David is the famous King David.[57]

In some receptor languages adaptations of this type of genealogy must be made because of the normal direction for designating relations. For example, in some languages one counts back from a particular person; hence, the genealogy would begin with David and count back, enumerating the various men back to Perez. On the other hand, it may be necessary in some languages to assume that Obed is the pivotal person and therefore count back to Perez and forward to David. Otherwise the whole time setting would need to be changed, thus relating the time to the author rather than to the story.

NOTES

TRANSLATING THE BOOK OF RUTH

1. With regard to the date of the book, not much can be deduced from the phrase "in the days when the judges ruled." Crucial in the discussion about the date are the relation between Ruth 4.7 and Deuteronomy 25.9, the few Aramaisms used, and the universal outlook of the book. See the introductions and commentaries on these questions. It is wise to adopt Bentzen's prudent judgment in connection with the time of composition: "The time from the later periods of the monarchy down into post-exilic days is the land of wide possibility, with which we have to reckon" (Aage Bentzen, Introduction to the Old Testament, Vol. II, Copenhagen, 1967, p. 185).

2. D. F. Rauber, "Literary Values in the Bible: the Book of Ruth," Journal of Biblical Literature 89 (1970), pp. 27-38; see particularly pp. 29 and 30.

CHAPTER 1

1. So Targum: "and it happened in the days in which the chiefs ruled" (negid negidayya').

2. See W. Gesenius and F. Buhl, Hebräisches und Aramäisches Handwörterbuch über das Alte Testament, 1949, s.v. 'erets.

3. Gesenius and Buhl, s.v. sadheh.

4. Compare Louis Pirot and Albert Clamer, La Sainte Bible, Tome III, Josué-Juges-Ruth-Samuel-Rois, Paris, 1955, ad loc., and F. M. Abel, Géographie de la Palestine, Tome I, Paris, 1933, pp. 278-281. Compare also NAB.

5. F. Brown, S. R. Driver, and C. A. Briggs, A Hebrew and English Lexicon of the Old Testament, Oxford, 1966, s.v. ghur.

6. For parallels of these proper names in the El-Amarna letters and the Ugarit tablets, as well as for the function of these proper names in the narrative, see the discussions in W. Rudolph, "Das Buch Ruth übersetzt und erklärt," Kommentar zum AT, XVI, 1962, ad loc.; M. Haller, "Die fünf Megilloth," Handbuch zum AT 1, 18, Tübingen, 1940, ad loc.; H. W. Hertzberg, Die Bücher Josua, Richter, Ruth, ATD 9, Göttingen, 1954, ad loc.; O. Eissfeldt, Einleitung in das Alte Testament, Tübingen, 1964, p. 651. Compare also M. Noth, Die israelitischen Personennamen, 1928, p. 10.

7. For an analysis of difficulties involved in transliterations, see E. A. Nida, Bible Translating, London, 1961, pp. 243-246, and Toward a Science of Translating, Leiden, 1964, pp. 193-195.

8. Haller, ad loc.

9. This is the idea given in the standard Hebrew dictionaries.

10. Tamisier in Pirot-Clamer, ad loc.; Gillis Gerleman, "Ruth—Das Hohelied," Biblischer Kommentar Altes Testament, Neukirchen, 1965, ad loc.

11. Ruth 1.3 and 5 are the only instances in the OT where the verb sha'ar is used with reference to a widow.

12. So Bible de Jérusalem and Edouard Dhorme in La Bible, l'Ancien Testament, Tome 2, Paris, 1959.

13. nasa' 'ishah, instead of the usual laqaḥ 'ishah, occurs in Ezra 10.44; 2 Chronicles 11.21; 13.21, and with ellipsis of 'ishah in Ezra 9.2, 12; Nehemiah 13.25; 2 Chronicles 24.3.

14. Orpah has usually been considered as a derivative of the root 'rph, of which the noun 'oreph ("neck") occurs several times in Hebrew as a figure of apostasy (Jeremiah 2.27; 32.33); but a derivation from a root 'phr (with metathesis), resulting in a meaning "mountain-goat," has seriously been proposed. As to Ruth, much has been deduced from the Syriac spelling found in the Peshitta re'ut, but elision of an 'ayin cannot easily be explained. A connection with a root rawah ("saturate, refresh"), as proposed by A. Bertholet (in Marti's Kurzer Handkommentar zum AT, 1898, ad loc.), is very doubtful, as well as a connection with Chaldaic werad ("rose"). The suggestion has even been made that the reversed reading of the name of Ruth, tur, meaning "turtledove," may be of significance! (Hertzberg, ad loc.). The usual explanation of the name Orpah already dates back to early rabbinic times as shown by D. Hartmann, Das Buch Ruth in der Midraschliteratur, Zürich, 1901. However, the etymologizing interpretation of a name is a common literary feature which tells us nothing about the correctness of the etymology. On the contrary, it is only a literary feature and/or an interpretative device of the expositors of a certain tradition. See James Barr, The Semantics of Biblical Language, Oxford, 1961, Chapter 6: "Etymologies and Related Arguments."

15. So the majority of LXX manuscripts and the Peshitta.

16. See E. A. Nida and C. R. Taber, The Theory and Practice of Translation, Leiden, 1969, p. 91; J. de Waard, "Do You Use 'Clean Language'?," The Bible Translator 22 (1971), pp. 107-115.

17. See particularly Brown-Driver-Briggs, s.v., with regard to the vowel pattern and its degree of certainty.

18. However, the Hebrew leḥem occurs also on a lower level of the taxonomy with the specific meaning "bread." On the other hand, in Arabic the related root lhm seems to occur only on such a lower level with the specific meaning "meat."

19. So Peshitta.

20. In Hebrew, the subject present in the verbal prefix (see Carl Brockelmann, Grundrisz der vergleichenden Grammatik der semitischen Sprachen I, Hildesheim, 1966, par. 260 Cb) has to be repeated pronominally when a second subject is added. See P. Joüon, Grammaire de l'hébreu biblique, Rome, 1947, par. 146c.

21. LXX has third person singular in the first verbal form but third person plural in the following verbs.

22. So the Syriac version. The third person plural is also found in some LXX manuscripts; the omission of "on the way" occurs also in the Old Latin.

23. So the Targum.

24. This is the reading of the Codex Alexandrinus and of some other LXX manuscripts.

25. So the Syriac version.

26. Herbert Hajek, "Heimkehr nach Israel, Eine Auslegung des Buches Ruth," Biblische Studien 33, Neukirchen, 1962, pp. 28-29.

27. This is the question asked by R. de Vaux, Les institutions de l'Ancien Testament I, Paris, 1961, p. 69.

28. This suggestion has been made by A. Lods, Israël des origines au milieu du VIIIe siècle, 1930, p. 219 (English translation by S. H. Hooke, Israel from Its Beginnings to the Middle of the Eighth Century, 1932. Page numbers are quoted according to the French edition.) A. Vincent (La Sainte Bible, le livre des Juges, le livre de Ruth, Paris, 1958, p. 152, note b) notes that each wife had her own tent and that the girls lived in the tent of their mother. According to E. F. C. Rosenmüller ("Judices et Ruth," Scholia in Vetus Testamentum, libri historici, Vol. II, 1835, ad loc.) and P. Joüon (Ruth, commentaire philologique et exégétique, 1953, ad loc.), the mention of the mother's house should have a sentimental value, and by virtue of this sentimental value it should make the argument stronger. Though this may be true, the stress on the connotative meaning can hardly be the only explanation of the formula.

29. So rightly W. Baumgartner, Hebräisches und Aramäisches Lexikon zum Alten Testament, Lieferung I, Leiden, 1967, s.v. ḥesed. The phrase ʾasah ḥesed is also found in Genesis 21.33; Joshua 2.12; Judges 1.24; 8.35; 1 Samuel 15.6; 20.8; 2 Samuel 3.8; 9.1,7; 10.2; 1 Chronicles 19.2.

30. Hebrew has literally: "The Lord give you that you may find a resting-place, each of you in the house of her husband." The syndetic combination of syntactically different clauses (see Joüon, par. 177h) in verse 9a already created difficulties for early translators. In a number of Greek and Syriac manuscripts, ḥesed has been added to lakem in order to get an easier syntactic construction. The Syriac reading "in the house of your fathers" may have been found ad hoc for the same reasons.

31. See Brown-Driver-Briggs, s.v. nasaʾ.

32. Compare E. Dhorme, Emploi métaphorique des noms de parties du corps, Paris, 1923, p. 136.

33. So the Syriac version.

34. See Brockelmann, Syntax, par. 294.

35. Tamisier translates correctly "retournez."

36. So LXX and Syriac version.

37. So in some Greek manuscripts: kai egenomēn lelakkōmenē andri. This is even true when their translation was based on a misreading ḥalilah for hallaylah.

38. The euphemism used in NEB, "if I were to marry this night," has the disadvantage of not focusing on sexual intercourse.

39. See M. Jastrow, A Dictionary of the Targumim, the Talmud Babli and Yerushalmi, and the Midrashic Literature, I, II, New York, 1950, s.v. ʾagan.

40. See Joüon, par. 160j and 161I.

41. Both interpretations are already present in the LXX tradition. For the elliptic comparison in the first, see Joüon, par. 141i.

42. See Gesenius-Buhl and Brown-Driver-Briggs, s.v. ʾod.

43. The Syriac version also has an extra expression, but a somewhat dif-

ferent wording: "she returned and went her way." The fact that both extra expressions have a different wording makes it highly improbable that they were originally part of the primitive Hebrew text, as suggested by Dhorme (ad loc.). We rather have to judge these extra expressions as good, early examples of the translation technique of making implicit information explicit.

44. LXX has "and Naomi said"; in the Syriac version we read: "and her mother-in-law said." Compare also Moffatt and NEB.

45. The Syriac translator of Ruth did not like the mention of pagan gods and therefore changed the expression into "to the house of her parents."

46. See the discussion in Nida, Bible Translating, 13.1.

47. LXX manuscripts and Syriac version read: return also yourself.

48. See P. Humbert, "Art et leçon de l'histoire de Ruth," Revue Théologique et Philologique 26 (1938), pp. 257-286.

49. The Targum even inserts here a short proselyte catechism. Some ancient versions lay more stress upon the declaration in using explicitly emphatic pronouns (LXX[B], Targum: "where you go yourself"; Syriac: "there I will be buried, I also") and emphatic locatives (some LXX manuscripts: "I will lodge there").

50. See Brown-Driver-Briggs s.v. phaga'.

51. So Joüon, par. 165a, note 3.

52. Compare the Latin equivalent found in Livy (i, 24, ad fin.) and quoted by J. A. Montgomery and H. Snyder Gehman, The Books of Kings, Edinburgh, 1960, p. 100: Tu, illo die, Iupiter, populum Romanum sic ferito, ut ego hunc porcum hic hodie feriam; tanto magis ferito quanto magis potes pollesque. See also J. Pedersen, Der Eid bei den Semiten, 1914.

53. See Gerleman, ad loc.; Brown-Driver-Briggs s.v. ki 1c. The deictic particle has asseverative force.

54. Again ancient translators already saw the necessity of making the participants explicit, as shown by the reading of LXX manuscripts and the Syriac in the first case "Naomi," and by that of some LXX manuscripts in the second case "Ruth."

55. See Baumgartner s.v. hom' : "ausser sich geraten." Same use of the verb with synecdoche of "city" in 1 Kings 1.45 and with synecdoche of the "earth" in 1 Samuel 4.5.

56. So rightly Joüon, par. 161b. Compare Tamisier's translation: "C'est donc Noémi!"

57. See Johs. Pedersen, Israel, Its Life and Culture, III-IV, London and Copenhagen, 1947, p. 665; A. Alt, "Der Gott der Väter" (Beitr. z. Wiss. vom AT, 3 Folge, Heft 12), 1929. According to B. D. Eerdmans (The Religion of Israel, Leiden, 1947, p. 20), Yahweh is identified in a few passages with Shaddai, but in others El Shaddai refers to the protecting genius of the family. In all other instances Shaddai should be distinguished from Yahweh. Only in a later period in which all divine powers were absorbed by Yahweh, Shaddai became equivalent with the God of the covenant. See also B. D. Eerdmans, Studies in Job, 1939, p. 12. One should not exclude the possibility that Ruth 1.20b contains an allusion

to Job 27.2. This could account for the use of Shaddai, which is found only in 1.20-21.

58. For the different proposals as to the possible derivations, as well as for the literature on the subject, see the dictionaries.

59. Accidentally, because English mar seems to be derived from a Germanic root marr- II. Compare R. Grandsaignes d'Hauterive, Dictionnaire des racines des langues européennes, Paris, 1948, s.v. marr- II.

60. RSV follows LXX, Syriac version, and Vulgate, all of them reading a piel of a verb 'anah III, meaning "to mishandle," "to afflict." However, the Hebrew 'anah I with its qal, meaning "to pronounce," "to testify," makes good sense. Moreover, only this verb can be constructed with the preposition be.

61. For the use of the wayyiqtol in this sense, see Joüon, par. 118i.

CHAPTER 2

1. See D. F. Rauber, art. cit., pp. 30-32.

2. Compare W. Baumgartner, s.v. ḥayil: "als Standesbezeichnung: (Gross-) Grundbesitzer" and G. Gerleman, op. cit., ad loc. See also E. Meyer, Die Israeliten und Nachbarstämme, 1906, pp. 428 f., 500.

3. See Johs. Pedersen, Israel, Its Life and Culture I-II, London and Copenhagen, 1946, pp. 46-60.

4. The Greek transliteration booz/s favors an interpretation "in him is power." Modern research, however, suggests a relation with Arabic baġz ("quickness"). See especially W. Baumgartner s.v. and M. Noth, op. cit., p. 228. The Hebrew word has to be distinguished from its homonym occurring in 1 Kings 7.21 and 2 Chronicles 3.17: Boaz, as a name of the left temple column. Only Baumgartner rightly makes a distinction between the two roots on the base of semantically obscure relations.

5. Compare Joüon, par. 114d, N. On the deprecative interjection -na', see par. 105c. Semantically, no politeness seems to be involved in its use.

6. For the Syriac translator also, this repetition seems to be superfluous. In 2.21, where he also omits "Moabitess," he is even joined by LXX and Vulgate.

7. The second verb in the sequence "set forth-went-gleaned" is omitted in most LXX manuscripts, Peshitta, and Vulgate.

8. Though NAB's translation, "The field she entered to glean after the harvesters happened to be the section belonging to Boaz of the clan of Elimelech," disregards the place of the disjunctive accent atnah.

9. Hebrew miqreh does occur in other places (1 Samuel 6.9; 20.26) with the meaning "accident," but the construction wayyiqer miqreh is typical of Ecclesiastes (see the dictionaries). This should warn one against making too artificial (and too modern!) a distinction between the meanings in Ruth and Ecclesiastes. Tamisier's statement (op. cit., ad loc.), "cette circonstance fortuite élimine tout plan préconçu," may be true on the sentence level; it is certainly not true on the level of the discourse. Gerleman (op. cit., ad loc.) first makes

the distinction between "chance" and "fate" and then abolishes the same distinction in saying that Yahweh dictates the "chance." He is nevertheless right, only not in his formulation, since he fails to reason on the two different levels, that of sentence and that of discourse. LXX in vocalizing miqreh instead of miqreha ("chance" for "her chance") and in reading thus periptomati (by "lucky chance") [see H. G. Liddell and R. Scott, A Greek-English Lexicon, Oxford, 1951, s.v.] may have been aware of the ambiguity of the Hebrew expression and may have solved the problem on the sentence level. On the other hand, some translations, though perhaps not consciously, operate on two levels at the same time. So Dhorme "sa chance voulut" and Jérusalem "sa chance la conduisit." This is a happy solution in French, but in a number of languages, where one cannot have an inanimate subject of an event, it cannot be applied.

10. There is no reason to see in these greetings an expression of a pious attitude (so Bertholet, op. cit., ad loc.) or to evaluate them as typical "harvest greetings" (so H. Gunkel, Ruth, Reden und Aufsätze, 1913, pp. 65-92). Compare Arabic allah ma'akum ("Allah be with you") and the answer allah yaḥphaḍak ("may Allah protect you"). In the two nominal phrases in Hebrew a verbal form with optative mood is implicit. See Joüon, par. 163b.

11. It is interesting to note that the Syriac translator in reading "peace with you" makes a type of cultural adaptation.

12. In some ancient versions, possessive constructions seem to have been considered as redundant in both cases. See Vulgate iuveni qui messoribus praeerat and LXX[A].

13. This is precisely the text according to the Targum.

14. For the translators of the Syriac version and the Vulgate, an explicit subject was clearly a redundant feature as well as the use of two verbs of saying: "he answered...and he said." Accordingly, they omitted the first verbal and nominal phrase. The same applies to a few LXX manuscripts.

15. Definite articles are found in many LXX manuscripts.

16. Compare G. Dalman, Arbeit und Sitte in Palästina, Vol. III, pp. 46 ff., 1964 (reprint of the 1928-42 edition).

17. The whole phrase "and gather among the sheaves" is lacking in the Syriac version and in the Vulgate. The Bible de Jérusalem follows partly this versional evidence in omitting "among the sheaves." Among the English translations, RSV, NEB, and Moffatt reproduce the Hebrew text. NAB's rendering "to gather the gleanings into sheaves" suggests a sequence of two related actions, but the translation is quite exaggerated. There is no indication that "gleanings" should be the implicit object of "to gather," and it is impossible to translate the Hebrew preposition be with "into." Among recent commentators, Gerleman (op. cit., ad loc.) is in favor of the omission of the prepositional phrase "among the sheaves." Others propose different changes in the Hebrew text. Joüon, Rudolph, and Haller (see their commentaries ad loc.) propose to read ba'amirim ("stalks") instead of ba'amarim ("sheaves"). However, Hertzberg (op. cit., ad loc.) is certainly right when he observes that this particular meaning of 'amir is very questionable and that this would be the only instance where the collective singular

noun ʿamir would have a plural suffix. However, his own proposal to read we'osephot instead of we'asaphti (this means reading "Garbensammlerinnen" ["gatherers of sheaves"] for "let me gather") is also subject to many objections. First, one would expect in such a case a connective construction we'osephot ʿamarim (without the preposition be), and then one would expect to find this construction at the end of the sentence, in any case after the preposition 'aḥare ("after").

18. The whole temporal phrase runs as follows: me'az habboqer we'ad-ʿattah zeh. For me'az with the meaning "since," see Brockelmann, Syntax, par. 251 f. ʿatta zeh forms a semantic unity; compare 1 Kings 17.24 and Baumgartner, s.v. zeh. This is understood rightly by the Vulgate. LXX "till evening" seems to be an interpretation which, for the most part, does not correspond with the time setting of the context. Dhorme does not seem to see that zeh forms a semantic unity with ʿatta and thus belongs to the temporal phrase. He takes the demonstrative pronoun wrongly as referring to meʿat. For the verse ending, the best solution is to follow Gerleman's suggestion in omitting the impossible habbayit ("house") as a dittography and to vocalize the verb with LXX and Syriac version as shabtah ("she stopped"). This is only a very small change. Moreover, it can be made acceptable on the basis that the Masoretes had to change the vocalization because of the presence of habbayit. LXX "in the field" is a correction of "in the house," though we must confess that this is implicitly the right location!

19. Compare C. Brockelmann, Hebräische Syntax, 1956, par. 54c.

20. So P. Humbert, art. cit., p. 267.

21. Compare also Translator's Handbook on Mark on 5.34 and Translator's Handbook on Luke on 8.48.

22. Compare Brown-Driver-Briggs s.v. dabaq. This dictionary has the advantage of giving the componential meanings of the verb. Baumgartner, on the contrary, groups the meanings according to the accompanying preposition, which in some cases is not semantically important. The componential meaning of the verb is the same in 2.21 and 2.23 in spite of the difference in the following prepositions. Baumgartner, in classing 2.23 with 1.14 because of the same prepositions used in both texts, completely disregards the componential meanings of the verb.

23. Gerleman, op. cit., ad loc., rightly observes that this is not a "Zustandssatz," and consequently he translates this sentence as follows: "Suche auf dem Felde."

24. NAB's rendering, "Watch to see which field is to be harvested," can only be the outcome of a complete misunderstanding. The only merit of the translation is that the passive transformation clearly and rightly suggests a different and implicit subject of "harvesting."

25. See Joüon, par. 112g. It is only in some of the individual translations in the commentaries that a correct rendering can be found. So Gerleman "Du sollst wissen, dasz ich den Knechten befehle" and Tamisier "Voici que j'ordonne ...."

26. So Targum, Syriac version, and Vulgate.

27. A good example of this is the Syriac version which simply states: "She fell on the ground and bowed before him."

28. hakkireni and nakriyyah. According to N. Nöldeke (Neue Beiträge zur semitischen Sprachwissenschaft, 1910, p.96) both items stem from the same root nkr with the meaning "als fremd, d.h. mit Aufmerksamkeit betrachten." Recent dictionaries, however, rightly make a semantic distinction between two roots nkr I and nkr II.

29. A better example of assonance is to be found in German in the text of the Zürcher Bible: "...und mich so freundlich beachtest? Ich bin ja nur eine Fremde."

30. Midrash Rabbah to Ruth, in referring to lehakkireni, already makes the future course of the story explicit: "she prophesied that he would know her in the way of all people" (i.e. as his wife).

31. This is the translation found in the Syriac version.

32. This is the text according to the Syriac version. The difficult construction "may your reward be full from the Lord, the God of Israel" has been transformed into "may he give you a full reward," whereas the nominal phrase "the God of Israel" has been added in apposition to the subject "Lord" in the first clause.

33. So Gerleman, op. cit., ad loc.

34. Compare A. Lods, op. cit., p. 532 f.: "Exceptionnellement Yahvé était représenté par le disque ailé, et on lui appliquait les métaphores de la théologie solaire."

35. Compare J. Ridderbos, De Psalmen I, Kampen, 1955, on Psalm 17.8.

36. See also Translator's Handbook on Luke on 13.34.

37. So in The Century Bible, a new edition based on the RSV, edited by John Gray, 1967, p. 414 f.

38. It is true that the word occurs with this meaning in 3.9, where Ruth asks Boaz to spread his skirt over her. But there the symbolism of the act implies both protection and union. On the other hand, it is only once stated in the OT that the Lord spreads his skirt over someone, but that is in the highly figurative speech of Ezekiel 16.8, where the relation between Yahweh and Israel is described in a wedding metaphor. On the contrary, the metaphor of the wings having Yahweh as the object of the comparison is quite frequent in poetic literature, though limited to the Psalms: 17.8; 36.8; 57.2; 61.5; 63.8; 91.4.

39. So rightly A. B. Ehrlich, Randglossen zur hebräischen Bibel VII, 1914, ad loc.; W. Rudolph and G. Gerleman, op. cit., ad loc.; compare also Baumgartner s.v. ḥen: "Ausdruck des Dankes."

40. For the translations, see NAB, Bible de Jérusalem, Dhorme. For the commentaries, especially those of Haller and Hertzberg. For the instantaneous aspect of the yiqtol form of the verb matsa', see Joüon, par. 113h and 111d. The only English translation doing justice to this aspect is the one by Moffatt: "I am finding favour with you, my lord...."

41. See now also Translator's Handbook on Luke on 1.6.

42. LXX reads: "See, I'll be as one of your servants," by deleting the negation marker lo'. In an effort not to delete a word of the text, it has been proposed several times to change the vocalization into lu', a particle with the meaning "if only," "oh that!" or "would that!" The whole results in a translation such

as is found in NAB: "would indeed that I were a servant of yours!" A similar translation has been proposed in a note in NEB (it is impossible to know the source of the translation in the NEB). Haller, op. cit., ad loc., is in favor of this interpretation, whereas more recent commentators are rightly unwilling even to change the vocalization of the Hebrew text.

43. In many LXX manuscripts the time setting is part of Boaz's speech: "It is now time to eat." It is always possible that ēdē hōra is a simple scribal error for tēj dē hōraj, a reading which occurs in some other LXX manuscripts. See also Joüon, par. 15k.

44. Compare J. Löw, Die Flora der Juden, I, 1924, pp. 102 ff., and G. Dalman, op. cit., III, p. 18, and IV, p. 388. The Syriac reading halba ("milk") can be interpreted as a scribal error for halla ("vinegar"). Such an error may have had a cultural background, as the custom described in Ruth 2.14 was not widespread. This is the only allusion to it in the Old Testament.

45. A parallel solution is to be found in the Bible de Jérusalem: "trempe ton morceau dans la piquette."

46. So Ḥagigah 22b (Talmud). For other references see Jastrow, s.v. tsabat.

47. So LXX, Vulgate. The Greek verb bounizō (which is found only in LXX Greek) may translate a Hebrew verb tsabar. It should, however, be noted that LXX uses a form of the same verb bounizō to translate the Hebrew noun tsebatim in 2.16. So it is not to be excluded that the Greek translator of Ruth thought of a verbal root tsbt in spite of its nonoccurrence in Biblical Hebrew. The Chaldaic form of the verb (tsebat) is attested in the Talmud (Ḥullin 60a) with the meaning "to present." Could the Greek translator have thought of such a meaning and could he have marked the quantity which was presented by way of interpretation? The object alphiton may also have influenced the translation of the verb! The reading of the Vulgate congessit may come from the Greek.

48. So e.g. Bible de Jérusalem: "et Booz lui fit aussi un tas de grains rōtis."

49. So e.g. R. Tamisier, op. cit., ad loc.

50. Compare Gerleman (op. cit., ad loc.), who refers to Ugaritic mṣbṭm ("pair of tongs") and Arabic and Ethiopic ḍabaṭa ("to hold firmly").

51. Compare Dalman, op. cit., III, p. 265 f.

52. See Joüon, par. 111g and 113l.

53. See also Dalman, op. cit., III, p. 39 f., p. 42, p. 48 f.; H. Vogelstein, Landwirtschaft in Palästina zur Zeit der Mišnäh, 1894, p. 61, p. 74 f. Compare also J. G. Wetzstein in Zeitschrift für Ethnologie, 1873, p. 273. Vulgate: etiam si vobiscum metere voluerit ("even if she wants to harvest with you") seems to have taken haʿamarim personally as a participle of a verb ʿamar. It is interesting to note that such a verb does not occur in Biblical Hebrew, though it is quite common in late Hebrew, where it seems to have the generic sense of "to harvest" and the specific meaning of "to bind and pile sheaves." See references in Jastrow, s.v. Compare also the reading of the Vetus Latina: inter manuatores.

54. Hebrew has an absolute infinitive followed by an imperfect of the same

verb shalal, which occurs only here in the Old Testament. For the absolute infinitive having the form of the construct infinitive, see Joüon, par. 123q. The emphasis on the action is stronger when the infinitive is placed before the finite form. See Joüon, par. 123d. LXX translated the verbal forms twice, probably to mark the two events of "holding in one's hand" and "throwing sideways." In the second case, some minuscules have a deviating reading soreusate, from a verb meaning "to heap one thing on another," which might well be a translation of a Hebrew verb salal ("cast up").

55. See Dalman, op. cit., III, p. 92.

56. So LXX in using the Greek verb rabdizo.

57. So the Vulgate reading: et quae collegerat virga caedens et excutiens.

58. Compare P. Perdrizet's remark in Syria, 1938, p. 48: "Les moissonneurs de Syrie ne ramassent pas les gerbes en meules; ils battent le blé sitôt coupé au moyen de rouleaux de pierre ou de traîneaux garnis par-dessous de silex tranchants; ou, si la récolte est minime, avec une baguette, comme on le voit faire dans la Bible à Ruth la Moabite pour les épis qu'elle avait glanés."

59. So A. G. Barrois, Manuel d'archéologie biblique, I, II, 1939-1953. The reference here is to II, p. 250.

60. So e.g. R. Tamisier, op. cit., ad loc.

61. See R. de Vaux, op. cit., pp. 306,307. Our lack of knowledge condemns "tout essai de donner, pour la période de l'Ancien Testament, un tableau d'équivalence avec notre système moderne" (p. 306).

62. So Vulgate: invenit hordei quasi oephi mensuram id est tres modios.

63. The Syriac version states, in a qualitative way, "a full measure."

64. So LXX.

65. The reading found in the TEV is attested by two Hebrew manuscripts according to C. H. H. Wright, The Book of Ruth in Hebrew with a Critically Revised Text, 1864, ad loc. Moreover, this reading is followed by Syriac version and Vulgate.

66. So Brown-Driver-Briggs s.v. yatsaʾ ("food from one's cupboard").

67. So rightly Dhorme and Bible de Jérusalem.

68. So rightly Gerleman, op. cit., ad loc: "abgekürzte Redeweise, eigentlich, 'Wohin (bist du gegangen) und hast gearbeitet?'" For the hapax ʾanah = ʾan, see the dictionaries. NEB seems to render a meaning "whither" and seems to interpret "to do" rather erroneously as "to go" ("Which way did you go?"). Another possibility is that NEB makes the first kernel structure explicit and the second implicit because of its repetitive character. If this is how the translators came to this translation, both the method and the result could be acceptable, though an implicit kernel structure in Hebrew could scarcely be given this importance. The meaning "where" for ʾanah has rightly been defended by Baumgartner s.v. Stinespring's proposal (in JNESt. 3, p. 101) to translate ʾanah with "wherefore?" does not seem to make any sense in this particular context.

69. Compare E. A. Nida, God's Word in Man's Language, New York, 1952, p. 43.

70. So LXX, which reads: "And Ruth told her mother-in-law where she had worked."

71. See Joüon, par. 132 f.; Brockelmann, Hebr. Syntax, par. 107c.

72. In the LXX the relative clause may refer back to Boaz, or it may refer back to both the Lord and Boaz. One manuscript de Rossi and the Syriac and Old Latin versions read: "Blessed be the Lord." Very probably the rare meaning of the preposition le was no longer understood, or both of the existing formulae "Blessed be he by the Lord" and "Blessed be the Lord" were confused.

73. Hebrew has a plural suffixed form of the participle. See H. Bauer and P. Leander, Historische Grammatik der hebräischen Sprache, 1922, par. 252r.

74. For more recent literature we refer especially to J. J. Stamm, Er-lösen und Vergeben im Alten Testament, 1940, pp. 27 ff.; A. R. Johnson, "The Primary Meaning of gaʾal," VT, Suppl. I (1953), pp. 67 ff.; and A. Jepsen, "Die Begriffe des Erlösens im Alten Testament" (in Festgabe für Rudolf Hermann z. 70. Geburtstag: "So lange es 'heute' heiszt"), 1957, pp. 153-163.

75. So in LXX, Vulgate, and Syriac version.

76. So LXX and Syriac version.

77. Compare Hertzberg, op. cit., ad loc.

78. So Joüon, par. 157a N: "(il y a) encore (ceci) qu'il a dit." Differently Gerleman, op. cit., ad loc.: "(Ich musz) noch (hinzufügen)." NEB: "And what is more..." seems to intensify the following statement, which is overtranslation. Even an omission (as in Moffatt) is semantically more justified.

79. So in some LXX manuscripts, the Ethiopic, Old Latin, and Armenian versions.

80. See the Century Bible, p. 416.

81. See Joüon, par. 141g.

82. So in the LXX, Vulgate, and Syriac version.

83. NAB is one of the rare exceptions in which this versional division is followed.

84. The alternative Hebrew reading (with different vocalization of the same consonants of the verbal form and change of ʾet- into ʾel-) found in two manu-scripts of Kennicott and in the Targum is followed by the Vulgate. Among the older translations, Luther is in favor of this reading, though he places it at the end of the second chapter. Among the newer translations, NAB apparently tries to combine both readings in stating "when she was back with her mother-in-law" at the beginning of chapter 3 (see note 83).

CHAPTER 3

1. For the use of wayyiqtol see Joüon, par. 118c, and already S. D. Luz-zatto, Grammatica ebraica, 1853, par. 1271.

2. Compare Joüon, par. 113m.

3. Compare Brown-Driver-Briggs s.v. manoah and manuḥah. See also Hertzberg, op. cit., ad loc.: "Wie 1.9 meint es konkret die Ehe."

4. For ʾasher as introduction of a consecutive clause, see Brockelmann, Syntax, par. 161b. Dhorme and NAB take ʾasher as introduction of a relative

clause: "a home...that will please you," an interpretation which is not generally followed.

5. According to Joüon, par. 89b, the feminine suffix -t in moda'at should have "une nuance intensive," so that the distinctive meaning of moda'at (compared with moda' Ruth 2.1) should be that of "near kinsman." Of the commentators, only Tamisier (op. cit., ad loc.) seems to support this interpretation. For the rare vocalization -anu of the possessive suffix, which may be due to the zaqef and the predicate character of the word, see Joüon, par. 94h; Bauer-Leander, par. 29m; and W. Gesenius-E. Kautzsch, Hebräische Grammatik, Leipzig, 1909[28], par. 91f.

6. For detailed information see Dalman, op. cit., I, p. 511 f.; III, pp. 127-129.

7. Contrary to Dalman, Hertzberg (op. cit., ad loc.) supposes that this operation took place in the afternoon, as the wind abates towards the evening. It is highly questionable, however, whether we can translate hallaylah with "afternoon." The greeting quoted by Hertzberg, exactly because of its anticipatory character, is no proof at all.

8. See also Translator's Handbook on Luke on 3.17.

9. An exception to this rule is the Bible de Jérusalem which translates correctly: "parfume-toi."

10. simlotayik is the reading of Q and 7 MSS[G].

11. Bethlehem was built on two hills. So for Haller (op. cit., ad loc.) the threshing floor was to be found on the lower hill. On the other hand, Hertzberg (op. cit., ad loc.), exploring local traditions about the "field of Boaz," thinks that the threshing floors of Bethlehem were to be found on the same spot where in our time the threshing floors of the village Beit Sahur, a village east of Bethlehem, are located. Midrash on Ruth only concludes from the use of the verb that the threshing floors were to be found on low spots.

12. See Joüon, par. 132c, note 2.

13. So Syriac version. Gerleman rightly sees that this variant reading does not presuppose a different Vorlage.

14. So rightly Gerleman, op. cit., ad loc.: "sich als Bittstellerin in seinen Schutz begeben."

15. Compare George A. F. Knight, Ruth and Jonah (The Torch Bible Commentaries), 1960[3], ad loc.: "Ruth's act in lying at Boaz's feet is not to be judged an indelicate act from our standard of ethical thinking. Such was the accepted manner in which a woman could propose marriage to a man." However, it surely was a hazardous act from the standard of Jewish ethical thinking. As we have to do with an isolated instance in the Old Testament, it may be going too far to speak of an "accepted manner."

16. For H. G. May (JRAS, 1939, pp. 75 ff.) and W. E. Staples (The Book of Ruth, AJSL 53, 1937, pp. 153 ff.), this is an instance of sacred prostitution which took place at Bethlehem's high place. The six measures of barley which Boaz gave to Ruth are interpreted as the hire of a sacred prostitute. Needless to say that such an interpretation makes the whole story incoherent.

17. It must be said that most verbs in this verse are frequently used as euphemisms for sexual intercourse in other contexts as: yada', shakab, bo', galah. Though the noun margelot is only found once outside the book of Ruth (in Daniel 10.6, where it is no euphemism), it is easily associated with a noun as raglayim, which is used as a euphemism for the male sex organ in e.g. Exodus 4.25.

18. The Syriac translator did so in omitting the expression "uncovered" and in only stating: "lie down at his feet." The Targum has an additional phrase in the last part of the verse: "He will tell you through his wisdom what to do."

19. This variant reading is found in Q, in a number of manuscripts Kennicott de Rossi, and in the Ginsburg text. Moreover, it is also found in many Targum and Syriac manuscripts.

20. According to J. G. Wetzstein, it was unthreshed. See J. G. Wetzstein, "Die syrische Dreschtafel," Zeitschrift für Ethnologie 5, 1873, pp. 270-302. For the opposite opinion see Gerleman, op. cit., ad loc.

21. The Syriac translator made this information explicit in the following way: "And when he was quietly sleeping on the threshing floor...."

22. LXX[B] omits wattishkab; Peshitta gives a different interpretation: "she fell at his feet." Both versions omit Boaz's drinking!

23. A good example of this is N. H. Tur-Sinai (The Book of Job, Jerusalem, 1957, ad loc.), who after giving all the meanings in cognate languages, finally bases his translation on a parallel text elsewhere in Job.

24. The transitive meaning of Arabic lafata is "to twist," "to wring" (e.g. a man's neck). 'alfatu is a man with a powerful grasp, who hoists or wrings one who grapples with him. See E. W. Lane, Al-Qamusu, an Arabic-English Lexicon, 1863-93, s.v. Parallel meanings are found in other cognate languages as Aramaic and Syriac. On the other hand, in Accadian lapâtu usually means "to touch."

25. So the Targum.

26. See LXX kai etarachthē "and he was disturbed"; Vulgate et conturbatus est; Syriac watwah "he was struck."

27. On the other hand, it is surely for stylistic reasons that the Targum, Vulgate, and Syriac version changed the interjection into a (neutral) verbal form: "and he saw."

28. For 'amah with this meaning, see Baumgartner s.v. The same formula is already found in Ugaritic. See J. Gray, The Legacy of Canaan, 1965, p. 105.

29. For the reference to marriage see Deuteronomy 23.1 and Ezekiel 16.8. Compare also A. S. van der Woude (in THAT I, 1971, s.v. kanaf): "Als Rechtsbrauch wird er (i.e. der Zipfel des Gewandes) vom Manne über die erwählte Braut ausgebreitet." See also A. Jirku, Die magische Bedeutung der Kleidung in Israel, 1914, pp. 14 ff. Arabic parallels to the levirate marriage show that the near kinsman established his claim to the widow by throwing his garment over her. See W. R. Smith, Kinship and Marriage in Early Arabia, 1903, p. 105; G. Jacob, Altarabisches Beduinenleben, 1897, p. 58, and J. L. Burckhardt, Bemerkungen über die Beduinen und Wahaby, 1831, p. 213.

30. Haller (op. cit., ad loc.) translates "wings," but does not exclude in his commentary the possibility of the alternative reading. For him the ambiguity may even have been intended by the author. Hertzberg (op. cit., ad loc.) may be right in seeing in the reading "wings" a euphemism.

31. So rightly H. H. Rowley, "The Marriage of Ruth," Harvard Theological Review XL, 1947, p. 92. Rowley (note 57) quotes J. Lewy who (RHR cx, 1934, pp. 31 ff.) cites Assyrian evidence showing that the skirt of the garment stood for the personality of the wearer, and especially for his honor. This evidence would signify that Boaz extended the cover of his position and person to Ruth.

32. See Joüon, par. 132 f.

33. The reversed order is already found in the Syriac version.

34. See Gerleman, op. cit., ad loc.: "Sie soll auch keine Angst haben, dasz man 'im Tor' wegen ihrer moabitischen Herkunft Einwände erheben wird."

35. A good example of this is the translation of the Vulgate: omnis populus qui habitat intra portas urbis meae. It is not completely clear how the Greek translation has to be evaluated. LXX has pasa phulē laou mou, in which phulē ("race, tribe") could be a defective writing of pulē ("gate"). This is, for example, Gerleman's interpretation. On the other hand, phulē may have the meaning of "a body of men united by local habitation" (see Liddell-Scott s.v.), so that the Greek could be translated as "the whole body of my people" (i.e. "towns people"). Is pulē/phulē an intentional pun of the Greek translator? Compare, however, the Syriac reading: "the whole tribe of our people."

36. The Targum's qualification tsaddiqta' presupposes a meaning "pious" in view of the following addition: "and you have the power to bear the yoke of the divine commandments."

37. That is why Staples (op. cit., pp. 62 ff.) states that Naomi did know about his existence. However, for that purpose he has to change the text of Ruth 2.20 into "he is not our go'el" and that of Ruth 3.12 into "I am not really your go'el," but these renderings are very unnatural and not convincing.

38. Against Humbert, art. cit., ad loc.

39. Probably Ruth, when infringing the rights of the closer relative, could even have been charged with adultery. See Rowley's comparison with the Tamar case, art. cit., p. 93 f.

40. See Dalman, op. cit., III, p. 127.

41. In the Haggada, the Hebrew tob ("good"), which is found in the normal subject position, is taken as the proper name of the closer relative and this Tob has been made an elder brother of Boaz ! This interpretation presupposes an ellipsis of the apodosis (compare Joüon, par. 167r).

42. The formula in this particular form occurs 41 times in the Old Testament, 30 of which are in the books of Judges to 2 Kings. It is already found in the Lachish ostraca. See H. Donner-W. Röllig, Kanaanäische und aramäische Inschriften, I, Texte, 1966, nr. 193, line 9 and nr. 196, line 12.

43. J. Pedersen, Israel, Its Life and Culture, I-II, p. 407.

44. J. Pedersen, idem, III-IV, p. 450.

45. So the Syriac translator, who makes the setting explicit in adding after the verbal form "she got up": "in the morning when it was still dark."

46. For reasons of a more logical sequence, the Syriac translator made Ruth the subject of the utterance: "she said to him, 'Nobody should know that I came to you on the threshing floor.'"

47. This is the interpretation found in the Targum.

48. So Vulgate: et dixit Booz, cave ne quis noverit quod huc veneris.

49. This is the interpretation of some modern commentators as Haller and Gerleman (op. cit., ad loc.).

50. Rudolph (op. cit., ad loc.) has already seen this and he inserts bidbare ("at his command") after wattaqom ("she got up"). In this he is followed by Haller. Hertzberg, on the other hand, thinks that such an operation is not necessary. However, we should make a distinction between an emendation of the source text and the necessity of making implicit information explicit in translation. The former is not justified, the latter is obligatory.

51. This is the reading according to the LXX.

52. Compare already some LXX manuscripts and Syriac version, both of which read "he said to her." Other LXX manuscripts are even more specific: "he said to Ruth."

53. See Gesenius-Buhl, s.v. mitpaḥat: "ein groszes Umschlagetuch der Frauen." Compare also Dalman, op. cit., V, p. 332.

54. See Joüon, par. 142n; Brockelmann, Syntax, par. 85e.

55. Especially Joüon and Brockelmann.

56. That is the interpretation of the Targum, which is followed by Hertzberg. According to some scholars, a sturdy female peasant could carry that much. However, even for the Targum translator the weight must have been exceptional, for he states that God gave Ruth the strength to carry this burden because she would be the ancestress of the Messiah!

57. So Gerleman, Haller, and the Century Bible, op. cit., ad loc. This opinion is also shared by A. Vincent (op. cit., ad loc.) and very probably by Th. J. Meek (in Smith-Goodspeed), where "six homers" must be a transcription error for "six omers," the ḥomer being equal to 10 ephah!

58. Of modern translations only Dhorme and NAB make Boaz the subject of the event. Compare NAB: "he poured out six measures of barley, helped her lift the bundle and left for the city." Of modern commentators only Gerleman seems to be in favor of this more difficult reading. The feminine preformative is found in 17 manuscripts Kennicott and in 37 manuscripts de Rossi and is further supported by the Syriac version and the Vulgate.

59. The Syriac version seems to have taken the question in this sense, as is clear from the answer added to the text: "And she answered her, 'I am Ruth.'" That even early translators had difficulties in understanding the Hebrew, can be seen from the LXX^B text, which simply omits the question and maintains the word "daughter." Gerleman (op. cit., ad loc.) takes mi as a question marker in the sense of Latin num, and defends this use in referring to Amos 7.2,5. Compare also H. S. Nyberg, Hebreisk Grammatik, 1952, par. 28f., note 2.

60. Such a meaning is already attested in the Rash Shamra texts: bʿl mt...

my hmlt 'atr b'l ("Baal is dead.... What of the multitudes, the followers of Baal?").

61. As suggested by Haller, op. cit., ad loc.

CHAPTER 4

1. For this see Brockelmann, Syntax, par. 41.

2. So Syriac version.

3. Compare also J. de Waard, "Quelques problèmes de traduction dans le livre des Psaumes," Flambeau 21, 1969, pp. 23-30, ad Psalm 9.14; idem, "The Translation of Some Figures of Speech from Psalms in Bamiléké and Bamoun," TBT 20, 1969, p. 144.

4. This has been denied by S. R. Driver, Critical and Exegetical Commentary on Deuteronomy, 1896, p. 285, and by L. M. Epstein, Marriage Laws in the Bible and the Talmud, 1942, pp. 86 ff., who distinguishes levirate marriage and ge'ullah marriage and who identifies the marriage of Ruth with the latter.

5. See the very thorough discussion in Rowley, art. cit. Compare also R. de Vaux, op. cit., I, p. 41.

6. See Baumgartner s.v. 'almoni.

7. So Hertzberg, op. cit., ad loc.

8. So Rudolph, Haller, Gerleman, Century Bible.

9. The LXX uses a Greek vocative kruphie, but this appears to be a literal rendering, quite unnatural in Greek. The Syriac translator reading, "And he said to him: Why?", must have misunderstood the Hebrew completely, as he also misunderstood the expression in the two other Old Testament places. Vulgate has a free rendering, vocans eum nomine suo, which has been followed by NAB and NEB: "calling him by name"!

10. An exception could be made in the case of Arabic where a common expression as shu'smuk ("what is your name?") or ya fulani is used. Compare also Brockelmann, Grundrisz II, par. 44, for other Semitic parallels.

11. See also R. de Vaux, op. cit., I, p. 108 f.; p. 212 f.

12. This is the opinion of Rowley, art. cit., p. 94 f.

13. So H. Greszmann, Haller, Hertzberg, Century Bible, and the majority of modern translations.

14. See Brockelmann, Syntax, par. 41d. An additional argument is that this use of the perfect is found in other legal procedures, e.g. in Genesis 23.11. Early translators certainly read a perfect, though they did not rightly understand the meaning: LXX hē dedotai; Syriac "Naomi has sold to me."

15. See Baumgartner, s.v. galah. Compare also Accadian uznā puttu and Dhorme, Emploi métaphorique, p. 89.

16. LXX seems to give a literal translation of the Hebrew: apokalupsō to ous sou. It is highly questionable, however, whether this is idiomatic Greek.

17. With many Hebrew manuscripts, Targum, Syriac version, LXX, and

Vulgate, one should read the second person singular instead of the third person singular.

18. See Joüon, par. 112f. A firm, definite answer should be expressed by the qatal form. Compare Haller's translation: "Ich will es schon lösen," or Bible de Jérusalem: "Oui, je veux bien racheter."

19. With qere one should read qanitah and with the Old Latin, Syriac, and Vulgate one should read we'et instead of me'et, a scribal error probably due to dittography.

20. L. Köhler ("Ruth," Schweizerische Theologische Zeitschrift 37, 1920) wants to omit the whole phrase "and from Ruth the Moabitess," arguing that the dead man concerned is Elimelech and the widow who has to be married is Naomi. In this he is followed by Haller. Already Volz (TLZ 26, 1901, cols. 348 f.) was of the opinion that in the original form of the story Naomi married Boaz. However, this view is unacceptable. Even Joüon (op. cit., p. 10) may not be right in stating that Ruth replaced Naomi legally. Finally, the nearest relative to Elimelech was also the nearest relative to Mahlon, and the levirate marriage could only make sense in relation to the younger of the two widows.

21. This is the text of Targum, Syriac version, and LXX. Even if this was not the original Hebrew text, it is clearly implicit information which has to be made explicit in translation.

22. A piel instead of a hiphil or palel form as we should expect. Compare Gesenius-Kautzsch, par. 72m. Moreover, the verbal form shows clearly Aramaic influences; see Joüon, par. 80h.

23. So A. R. S. Kennedy, The Book of Ruth, 1928, p. 57, and also G. A. Cooke, The Book of Ruth, 1918, p. 15.

24. Parallels to this extent have been cited from India, Egypt, and the Nuzi texts. See the literature quoted in Rowley, art. cit., notes 37-40. See also J. M. Mittelmann, Der altisraelitische Levirat, 1934, p. 21.

25. For the complicated relationship between Ruth 4.7 and Deuteronomy 25.9, see especially Rowley, art. cit., p. 86.

26. So LXX and Arabic version.

27. So Dhorme, op. cit., ad loc.

28. This seems to be Haller's opinion.

29. Apart from TEV, no modern translation consulted has this reading.

30. It will be necessary to understand with one manuscript of Wright, LXX, Syriac and Vulgate: "and to all the people."

31. See Joüon, par. 112f.: "j'acquiers (hic et nunc, par mes paroles)."

32. Semantically, the "cutting off of the name" remains in the same domain as the "cutting off of hope" (Proverbs 23.18; 24.14). See Kutsch's article in THAT I, s.v. krt. On the other hand, shem is sometimes synonymous to zera', so that "to cut off a name" means "to extirpate a family." However, in this connection the verb krt is only used once, Isaiah 14.22.

33. This is the reading found in the LXX, defended by Joüon, op. cit., ad loc., and followed by Bible de Jérusalem.

34. So rightly Gerleman, op. cit., ad loc.

35. See Baumgartner, s.v. banah, and A. R. Hulst, ibidem (in THAT).

36. So Bible de Jérusalem: "Deviens puissant en Ephrata," Gerleman, Haller, Hertzberg.

37. So already Vulgate: exemplum virtutis, Gesenius-Buhl and Brown-Driver-Briggs s.v. ḥayil, NEB.

38. So in one form or another RSV, NAB, Smith-Goodspeed, Dhorme. See also Baumgartner s.v. ḥayil: "zu Reichtum kommen."

39. So Luther who translates: "wachse sehr." Haller appears to be in favor of this translation, and Baumgartner (ibidem: Kindersegen) seems to leave this possibility of translation open.

40. So rightly Brown-Driver-Briggs s.v. qara. There is no need to change the Hebrew text into weniqra shimka (Kittel) or into qeneh shem (Century Bible). LXX: kai estai onoma seems to be a good idiomatic translation as well as Vulgate: et habeat celebre nomen in Bethleem. Some Greek manuscripts, however, give a literal translation: kalesai (imp.). The Syriac translator did not understand the meaning at all: "and call its name (scil. the name of E.) Bethlehem."

41. See H. Granquist, Marriage Conditions in a Palestinian Village II, Helsinki, 1935, pp. 120, 131 ff.

42. There is a problem here already and again in the genealogy where Ruth's child is likewise presented as the child of Boaz. Though highly hypothetical, Rowley's solution is very ingenious (art. cit., pp. 97-99). He thinks it probable that Boaz's wife was dead and he himself childless. But then Ruth's first child would be the child of Mahlon by legal fiction, and also the child of Boaz by actual paternity. In the case of a legal marriage with Ruth, the same child would be Boaz's as well as Mahlon's heir. This solution has the advantage of accommodating all the facts and makes any surgical treatment of the text unnecessary.

43. The words "and she became his wife" are lacking in LXX[B] and in the Ethiopic version, very probably because the translators were aware of the tautology. The same is true for Syr[h]: "And Boaz took Ruth as wife." This is also the reading preferred by Haller, though he gives no arguments for his preference.

44. See the discussion in J. de Waard, "Do you use 'clean language'?" The sentence "and he went in to her" is also lacking in the versions mentioned in note 43. Is this an attempt to "purify" the text, or is this merely implicit information in the light of what follows?

45. LXX kai kalesai to onoma sou relates to Naomi.

46. The Syriac translator (translating "your town" for "your old age") probably misread the Greek polian as polin. So G. Janichs, Animadversiones criticae in vers. Syriacam Peschitthonianam librorum Kohelet et Ruth, Marburg, 1869, ad loc.

47. See especially Baumgartner s.v. ḥeq.

48. See L. Köhler, "Die Adoptionsform von Ruth 4.16," ZAW 29 (1909), pp. 312-314; Gerleman, op. cit., ad loc.

49. So Lods, op. cit., p. 220 f.

50. So de Vaux, op. cit., p. 86.

51. So Brown-Driver-Briggs, Köhler, Baumgartner, Tamisier, and all modern English translations.

52. So Rudolph, Haller, Hertzberg, Luther, Zürcher, Bible de Jérusalem, Dhorme.

53. So the Syriac version. It should, however, be noted that such a re-structuring may destroy the traces of a more primitive text in which (according to the typical Hebrew style of name giving) instead of shem another name fig-urged, alluding to yullad ben lena omi, something like Yibleam (Gunkel, op. cit., ad loc.) or Ben Noam (Eiszfeldt, op. cit., p. 649).

54. S. Öttli (in Strack-Zöckler's Kurzgefaszte Kommentar, 1889, ad loc.) and Bertholet (op. cit., ad loc.) explain the name as "ganz für sie da." This is, however, questionable. It would be more probable to take it in the sense "wor-shiper" as a hypocoristic, in which the following name of the divinity has been omitted (so Dhorme, op. cit., ad loc.).

55. For many scholars the genealogy is a later addition which is even in-consistent with the preceding story. So E. König, Einleitung in das AT, 1893, p. 287; A. Bertholet, op. cit., ad loc.; S. R. Driver, Introduction to the Litera-ture of the OT, 1913, p. 455 f.; L. B. Wolfenson, The Book of Ruth, AJSL 27, 1910-11, p. 293; Joüon, op. cit., ad loc.; Haller, op. cit., ad loc. For some, even 4.17b has to be considered as a later addition. See O. Eissfeldt, Einleitung, pp. 648-650; F. Dijkema, Ruth 4.17-22, in NThT 24, 1935, pp. 111-118. Other scholars, while admitting the secondary character of the genealogy taken from 1 Chronicles 2.4-15 or from its source, do not see an inconsistency with the ear-lier part of the book. So A. Bentzen, op. cit., II, p. 183. Hertzberg and Gerle-man, op. cit., ad loc. On the other hand, some scholars consider the genealogy as an integral part of the book, revealing the final purpose of the story. So K. F. Keil, Lehrbuch der historisch-kritischen Einleitung, 1873, p. 437; L. Fillion, in Vigouroux, Dictionnaire de la Bible, V, 1912, cols. 1280 f.; Tamisier, op. cit., ad loc.

56. So Gerleman, op. cit., par. 6: "Sinn und Zweck des Buches."

57. With LXX[A], Syriac version, Vetus Latina and Vulgate A and ⊕.

GLOSSARY

accentual system. Added to the consonants of Hebrew are two sets of markings. One includes the vowel markings and the other indicates stresses, pauses, and the grammatical relationships between words. "Hebrew accentual system" often refers to both types of markings but may, in some contexts, indicate only the latter type.

adjective is a word which limits, describes, or qualifies a noun. In English, "red," "tall," "beautiful," "important," etc. are adjectives.

adverb is a word which limits, describes, or modifies a verb, an adjective, or another adverb. In English, "quickly," "soon," "primarily," "very," etc. are adverbs.

attributive is a term which limits or describes another term. In "the big man ran slowly," the adjective "big" is an attributive of "man" and the adverb "slowly" is an attributive of "ran." See adjective and adverb.

causative relates to events and indicates that someone caused something to happen, rather than that he did it himself. In "John ran the horse," the verb "ran" is a causative, since it was not John who ran, but rather it was John who caused the horse to run.

classifier is a term used with another term (often a proper noun) to indicate what category the latter belongs to. "Town" may serve as a classifier in the phrase "town of Bethlehem" and "river" as a classifier in "river Jordan."

cognate languages are those which are closely related and have many features of grammar and vocabulary which are similar. French and Spanish are cognate languages, as also are English and German.

conjunctions are words which serve as connectors between words, phrases, clauses, and sentences. "And," "but," "if," "because," etc. are typical conjunctions in English.

context is the relevant part of a message in which a particular form occurs. In "poor John was sick yesterday," the context of "John" is "poor...was sick yesterday." The context of a term often affects its meaning, so that it does not mean exactly the same thing in one context that it does in another.

discourse is the connected and continuous communication of thought by means of language, whether spoken or written. The way in which the elements of a discourse are arranged is called discourse structure. Direct discourse is the reproduction of the actual words of one person which are embedded in the discourse of another person. For example, "He declared, 'I will have nothing to do with this man.'" Indirect discourse is the reporting of the words of one person which is embedded in the discourse of another person in an altered grammatical form. For example, "He said he would have nothing to do with that man."

ellipsis (plural ellipses) or elliptical expression refers to words or phrases normally omitted in a discourse when the sense is perfectly clear without them. In the following sentence, the words within brackets are elliptical: "If [it is] necessary [for me to do so], I will wait up all night." What is elliptical in one language may need to be expressed in another.

euphemism or euphemistic expression is a mild or indirect term used in the place of another term which is felt to be impolite, distasteful, or vulgar. For example, "to pass away" is a euphemism for "to die."

explicit refers to information which is expressed in the words of a discourse. This is in contrast to implicit information. See implicit.

figurative expression or figure of speech is the use of words in other than their literal or ordinary sense, in order to suggest a picture or image or for some other special effect. Metaphors and similes are figures of speech.

first person. See person.

footnotes. See marginal helps.

idiom or idiomatic expression is a combination of terms whose meanings cannot be derived by adding up the meanings of the parts. "To hang one's head," "to have a green thumb," and "behind the eight ball" are English idioms. Idioms almost always lose their meaning completely when translated from one language to another.

imperative refers to forms of a verb which indicate commands or requests. In "go and do likewise," the verbs "go" and "do" are imperatives. In most languages imperatives are confined to the grammatical second person; but some languages have corresponding forms for the first and third persons. These are usually expressed in English by the use of "may" or "let." For example, "May we not have to beg!" "Let them eat cake!"

implicit refers to information that is not formally represented in a discourse, since it is assumed that it is already known to the receptor. This is in contrast to explicit information, which is expressed in the words of a discourse.

levirate marriage, — right. See the comments on the latter part of Ruth 2.20 (pp. 42-43) and on Ruth 4.5 (p. 68).

liturgical refers to liturgy, that is, public worship; more particularly to the prayers, responses, etc. which are often expressed in traditional or archaic language forms.

marginal helps in Bible Society usage are notes, normally occurring on the same page as the text and providing purely objective, factual information of the following types: alternative readings (different forms of the source-language text), alternative renderings (different ways of rendering the source-language text), historical data, and cultural details, all of which may be necessary for a satisfactory understanding of the text. Notes which are doctrinal or homi-

letical interpretations of the text are excluded from Scriptures published by
the Bible Societies.

markers are features of a discourse which signal some particular structure.
For example, words for speaking may mark the onset of a direct discourse,
a phrase such as "once upon a time" may mark the beginning of a fairy story,
and certain features of parallelism are the dominant markers of poetry.

Masoretes. Jewish scholars who, prior to the tenth century A.D., edited the
Hebrew Old Testament text to insure its correctness.

message is used in two senses: (1) the form of language used to communicate
information and (2) the information itself. Normally, the context will indicate
which of these meanings is intended.

metaphor is likening one object to another by speaking of it as if it were the
other, as "flowers dancing in the breeze." Metaphors are the most commonly
used figures of speech and are often so subtle that a speaker or writer is not
conscious of the fact that he is using figurative language. See simile.

noun is a word used as the name of a person, thing, quality, action, etc. In English, "man," "tree," "justice," "repentance," etc. are nouns. A noun may
function as the subject or the object of a verb. See proper name.

optative means expressing desire or choice. This is indicated in some languages
by certain verb forms.

paratactic construction is the combination of two statements without the use of
connecting words such as "and," "but," "if," "while," "which," etc.

participle is a verbal adjective, that is, a word which retains some of the char-
acteristics of a verb while functioning as an adjective. In "singing waters"
and "painted desert," "singing" and "painted" are participles.

particle is a small word whose grammatical form does not change. In English
the most common particles are prepositions and conjunctions.

passive. See voice.

perfect tense is a form of a verb which indicates an action already completed
when another action occurs.

person, as a grammatical term, refers to the speaker, the person spoken to,
or the person(s) or thing(s) spoken about. First person is the person(s) or
thing(s) speaking ("I," "me," "my," "mine"; "we," "us," "our," "ours").
Second person is the person(s) or thing(s) spoken to ("thou," "thee," "thy,"
"thine"; "ye," "you," "your," "yours"). Third person is the person(s) or
thing(s) spoken about ("he," "she," "it," "his," "her," "them," "their," etc.).
The examples here given are all pronouns, but in many languages the verb
forms distinguish between the persons and also indicate whether they are singular or plural.

[105]

play on words in a discourse is the use of the similarity in the sounds of two words to produce a special effect.

plural refers to the form of a word which indicates more than one. See singular.

preposition is a word (usually a particle) whose function is to indicate the relation of a noun or pronoun to another noun, pronoun, verb, or adjective. Some English prepositions are "for," "from," "in," "to," "with."

pronominal refers to pronouns.

pronouns are words which are used in place of nouns, such as "he," "him," "his," "she," "we," "them," "who," "which," "this," "these," etc.

proper name or proper noun is the name of a unique object, as "Bethlehem," "Jordan," "Boaz." However, the same proper name may be applied to more than one object. For example, besides Bethlehem in Judah, the scene of the Book of Ruth, there is a village in Zebulun called Bethlehem (Joshua 19.15).

receptor is the person receiving a message. The receptor language is the language into which a translation is made. The receptor culture is the culture of the people who speak the receptor language.

redundancy is the expression of information which is entirely predictable from the context. Such information is said to be redundant.

restructure is to reconstruct or rearrange. See structure.

second person. See person.

semantic refers to meaning. Semantics is the study of the meaning of language forms. In contrast to grammar, which classifies words as nouns, verbs, etc., according to how they are used, semantics classifies words according to their meaning.

Semitic refers to a family of languages which includes Hebrew, Aramaic, and Arabic.

sentence is a grammatical construction composed of one or more clauses and capable of standing alone.

simile is a figure of speech which describes one event or object by comparing it to another, as "she runs like a deer," "he is as straight as an arrow." Similes are less subtle than metaphors in that they use "like," "as," or some other word to mark or signal the comparison.

singular refers to the form of a word which indicates one thing or person, in contrast to plural, which indicates more than one.

source language is the language in which the original message was produced. For the Book of Ruth, ancient Hebrew is the source language.

structure is the systematic arrangement of the form of language, including the ways in which words combine into phrases, phrases into clauses, and clauses into sentences. Because this process may be compared to the building of a house or a bridge, such words as structure and construction are used in reference to it. To separate and rearrange the various components of a sentence or other unit of discourse in the translation process is to restructure it.

style is a particular or characteristic manner in discourse. Each language has certain distinctive stylistic features which cannot be reproduced literally in another language. Within any language, certain groups of speakers may have their characteristic discourse styles, and among individual speakers and writers, each has his own style. Various stylistic devices are used for the purpose of achieving a more pleasing style. For example, synonyms are sometimes used to avoid the monotonous repetition of the same words, or the normal order of clauses and phrases may be altered for the sake of emphasis.

subjunctive refers to certain forms of verbs that are used to express an act or state as being contingent or possible (sometimes as wish or desire), rather than as actual fact.

synonyms are words which are different in form but similar in meaning, as "boy" and "lad." Expressions which have essentially the same meaning are said to be synonymous.

syntactic refers to syntax, which is the arrangement and interrelations of words in phrases, clauses, and sentences.

tense is usually a form of a verb which indicates time relative to a discourse or some event in a discourse. The most common forms of tense are past, present, and future.

third person. See person.

verbs are a grammatical class of words which express existence, action, or occurrence, as "be," "become," "run," "think," etc.

verbal has two meanings. (1) It may refer to expressions consisting of words, sometimes in distinction to forms of communication which do not employ words ("sign language," for example). (2) It may refer to word forms which are derived from verbs. For example, "coming" and "engaged" may be called verbals.

voice in grammar is the relation of the action expressed by a verb to the participants in the action. In English and many other languages, the active voice indicates that the subject performs the action ("John hit the man"), while the passive voice indicates that the subject is being acted upon ("the man was hit").

[107]

INDEX

[109]

[110]

recognition (recognize) 58
redeem (redeemer, redemption) 43, 64, 67, 69, 70, 77
refuge 34
relative 24, 42, 48, 53, 54, 55, 56, 57, 64, 65, 66, 67, 68, 70, 77
request (ask) 18, 25
responsibility 57
Revised Standard Version 2, 15, 26, 42, 45, 48, 49, 52, 59, 68
reward 34
rhetorical 14, 15, 21
rich 74; — and influential 24; — or poor 55

sad 20
sandal 70, 71
se'ah 59
seated 65
secrecy (secretly) 51, 52
security 78
Segond 10
sell (seller) 66, 70
Semitic 27
Septuagint 10, 16
servant 28, 29, 31, 35, 44, 45, 53, 58
seven 78
sexual 50, 54, 76, 78
Shaddai 20, 21
sheaves 29, 30, 38
shelter 30, 34
sir 35, 65
sister-in-law 16
skirts 34, 53, 54
Smith-Goodspeed 47, 48, 51, 52, 56, 59, 63, 65, 67, 68, 72, 74
speaking gently 35
suddenly 52
sun-disk 34

surprised 53
swear 58

taboo 10
take notice 32, 41
taking care 42, 43
temporal 27, 30, 36
threshing (threshing floor) 48, 49, 57, 58, 59
Today's English Version 2, 3, 6, 10, 11, 14, 15, 16, 20, 21, 27, 28, 29, 31, 32, 35, 37, 39, 40, 41, 42, 43, 44, 47, 48, 49, 50, 54, 55, 57, 58, 59, 60, 61, 65, 66, 67, 68, 70, 72, 74, 76, 77, 78, 79, 81
took care 79
town 56; whole — 20
transitional 1, 2, 3, 6, 22, 23, 30, 45, 46, 60, 65, 76
tribe 16, 18, 24, 33
trouble 21
turn out 61
turned over 52

visit 10

watch 31
water jars 32
weep (cry) 13, 16
widow 68
wife 68, 76
wings 34, 54
winnowing 48, 49, 57
witness (witnesses) 71, 73, 74
woman (women) 55, 56, 73, 77; young — 29, 75
worked (workers, working) 25, 30, 37, 44, 45, 48

Yahweh 10, 13, 20, 26, 35

[111]